Mutual Fund
Fact Book

42nd Edition

A guide to *trends*

and *statistics* in the

mutual fund industry

INVESTMENT COMPANY INSTITUTE®

Forty-Second Edition

ISBN 1-878731-32-7

About ICI

The Investment Company Institute (ICI) is the national association of the investment company industry. Its mission is to advance the interests of investment companies (mutual funds, closed-end funds, unit investment trusts, and exchange-traded funds) and their shareholders, to promote public understanding of investment companies, and to serve the public interest by encouraging adherence to high ethical standards by all elements of the business. As the only association of U.S. investment companies without regard to distribution method or affiliation, the Institute is dedicated to the interests of the entire investment company industry and all of its shareholders. The Institute represents members and their shareholders before legislative and regulatory bodies at both the federal and state levels, spearheads investor awareness initiatives, disseminates industry information to the public and the media, provides economic policy and other policy research, and seeks to maintain high industry standards.

The association was originally formed by industry leaders who supported the enactment of the Investment Company Act of 1940, legislation that provided the strong regulatory structure that has been responsible for much of the industry's success. Established in New York in 1940 as the National Committee of Investment Companies, the association was renamed the National Association of Investment Companies in 1941 and the Investment Company Institute in 1961. The Institute was relocated to Washington, DC in 1970.

For more information on the Institute, its members, and how mutual funds operate, visit www.ici.org.

Table of Contents

CHAPTER 4

CHAPTER 5

DATA SECTION

GLOSSARY AND INDEX

List of Figures

CHAPTER 4

Mutual Fund Ownership and Shareholder Characteristics

CHAPTER 5

Retirement and Education Savings Markets

CHAPTER 1

Organization and Features of Mutual Funds

A mutual fund is a type of investment company that gathers assets from investors and collectively invests those assets in stocks, bonds, or money market instruments. Through the collective investments of the mutual fund, each investor shares in the returns from the fund's portfolio while benefiting from professional investment management, diversification, liquidity, and other services.

How a Mutual Fund Is Organized

A mutual fund is organized either as a corporation or a business trust. Individuals and institutions invest in a mutual fund by purchasing shares issued by the fund. It is through these sales of shares that a mutual fund raises the cash used to invest in its portfolio of stocks, bonds, and other securities.

A mutual fund is typically externally managed: it is not an operating company with employees in the traditional sense. Instead, a fund relies upon third parties, either affiliated organizations or independent contractors, to carry out its business activities, such as investing in securities. The diagram on page 4 shows the principal service providers to a mutual fund and its shareholders.

Shareholders

Like shareholders of other companies, mutual fund shareholders have specific voting rights. These include the right to elect directors at meetings called for that purpose (subject to a limited exception for filling vacancies). Shareholders must also approve material changes in the terms of a fund's contract with its investment adviser, the entity which manages the fund's assets. Furthermore, funds seeking to change investment objectives or policies deemed fundamental must seek shareholder approval.

Shareholders are provided comprehensive information about the fund to help them make informed investment decisions. A mutual fund's prospectus describes the fund's goals, fees and expenses, investment strategies and risks, as well as information on how to buy and sell shares. The U.S. Securities and Exchange Commission (SEC) requires a fund to provide a full prospectus either before an investment or together with the confirmation statement of an initial investment. In addition, periodic shareholder reports, prepared at least every six months by funds, discuss the recent performance and include other important information, such as the fund's financial statements. By examining these reports, an investor can learn if a fund has been effective in meeting the goals and investment strategies described in the fund's prospectus.

Directors

A board of directors, elected by the fund's shareholders to govern the fund, is responsible for overseeing the management of fund business affairs. Because mutual fund directors are, in essence, looking out for shareholders' money, the law holds them to a very high standard.

Directors must exercise the care that a reasonably prudent person would take with his or her own business. They are expected to exercise sound business judgment, establish procedures, and undertake oversight and review of the performance of the investment adviser and others that perform services for the fund. As part of this fiduciary duty, a director is expected to obtain adequate information about items that come before the board in order to exercise his or her "business judgment," a legal concept that involves a good-faith effort by the director.

Independent Directors. Mutual funds are the only companies in America required by law to include independent directors, individuals that cannot have any significant relationship with the fund's adviser or underwriter so that they can provide an independent check on the fund's operations. Furthermore, effective January 2002, SEC rule changes require that a majority of most funds' boards of directors be independent.

Independent directors serve as watchdogs for the shareholders' interests and oversee a fund's investment adviser and others closely affiliated with the fund. This system of overseeing the interests of mutual fund shareholders has helped the industry avoid systemic problems and contributed significantly to public confidence in mutual funds.

Investment Advisers

An investment adviser manages the money accumulated in a mutual fund. The investment adviser invests the fund's assets on behalf of shareholders in accordance with a fund's objectives as described in a fund's prospectus.

Diversification. Fund managers invest in a variety of securities, providing fund shareholders with investment diversification. A diversified portfolio helps reduce risk by offsetting losses from some securities with gains in others. Mutual funds provide an economical way for the average investor to obtain the same kind of professional money management and diversification of investments that is available to large institutions and wealthy investors.

Investment advisers who oversee "actively managed" fund portfolios base their investment decisions on extensive knowledge and research of market conditions and the financial performance of individual companies and specific securities in the effort to meet or beat average market returns. As economic conditions change, the fund investment adviser may adjust the mix of its investments to adopt a more aggressive or a more defensive posture in meeting its investment objectives. Investment managers who oversee "passively managed" funds, typically try to track a market index—such as the S&P 500—by buying and holding all, or a large representative sample, of the securities in the index.

A fund investment adviser is subject to numerous standards and legal restrictions, especially regarding transactions between itself and the fund it advises. A written contract between a mutual fund and its investment adviser specifies the services the adviser performs. Most advisory contracts provide that the adviser receive an annual fee based on a percentage of the fund's average net assets (see *Management Fee* on page 15).

Administrators

Administrative services may be provided to a fund by an affiliate of the fund, such as the investment adviser, or by an unaffiliated third party. Administrative services include overseeing the performance of other companies that provide services to the fund and ensuring that the fund's operations comply with legal requirements. Typically, a fund administrator pays for office costs and personnel, provides general accounting services, and may also prepare and file SEC, tax, shareholder, and other reports.

The Structure of a Mutual Fund

Shareholders

Board of directors
Oversees the fund's activities, including approval of the contract with the management company and certain other service providers.

Mutual fund

Investment adviser
Manages the fund's portfolio according to the objectives and policies described in the fund's prospectus.

Principal underwriter
Sells fund shares, either directly to the public or through other firms.

Custodian
Holds the fund assets, maintaining them separately to protect shareholder interests.

Independent public accountant
Certifies the fund's financial statements.

Transfer agent
Executes transactions—such as orders to buy and sell fund shares—on behalf of fund shareholders, maintains records of those transactions and other shareholder account activity, and sends account information—such as fund statements and transaction confirmations—to shareholders.

Principal Underwriters

Most mutual funds continuously offer new shares to the public at a price based on the current value of fund net assets plus any sales charges (see *Liquidity* on page 7). Mutual funds usually distribute their shares through principal underwriters. Principal underwriters are regulated as broker-dealers and are subject to National Association of Securities Dealers, Inc. rules governing mutual fund sales practices.

Custodians

Mutual funds are required by law to protect their portfolio securities by placing them with a custodian. Nearly all mutual funds use qualified bank custodians. The SEC requires mutual fund custodians to segregate mutual fund portfolio securities from other bank assets.

Transfer Agents

A transfer agent is employed by a mutual fund to maintain records of shareholder accounts, calculate and disburse dividends, and prepare and mail shareholder account statements, federal income tax information, and other shareholder notices. Some transfer agents prepare and mail statements confirming shareholder transactions and account balances, and maintain customer service departments to respond to shareholder inquiries.

Other Features of Mutual Funds

Variety

There are four basic types of mutual funds: equity (also called stock), bond, hybrid, and money market. Equity funds concentrate their investments in stocks. Similarly, bond funds primarily invest in bonds. Hybrid funds typically invest in a combination of stocks, bonds, and other securities. Equity, bond, and hybrid funds are called long-term funds. Money market funds are referred to as short-term funds because they invest in securities that generally mature in about one year or less. Of the total $6.975 trillion invested in mutual funds at the end of 2001, $3.418 trillion was invested in equity funds, $925 billion in bond funds, $346 billion in hybrid funds, and $2.285 trillion in money market funds.

Mutual Funds Versus Other Types of Investment Companies

Mutual funds are considered "open-end" investment companies under federal law for two reasons. First, they are required to redeem (or buy back) outstanding shares at any time upon a shareholder's request, and at a price based on the current value of the fund's net assets. Second, although not required, virtually all funds continuously offer new fund shares to the public.

In addition to mutual funds, there are three other types of investment companies regulated under the Investment Company Act of 1940: closed-end funds, unit investment trusts, and exchange-traded funds.

A **closed-end fund** is an investment company that issues a fixed number of shares, which trade on a stock exchange or in the over-the-counter market. Assets of a closed-end fund are professionally managed in accordance with the fund's investment objectives and policies, and may be invested in stocks, bonds, or a combination of both. Like other publicly traded securities, the market price of closed-end fund shares fluctuates and is determined by supply and demand in the marketplace. For statistical information on closed-end funds, see page 100.

A **unit investment trust** (UIT) is a registered investment company that buys and holds a generally fixed portfolio of stocks, bonds, or other securities. "Units" in the trust are sold to investors, or "unit holders," who receive their proportionate share of dividends or interest paid by the UIT investments. Unlike other investment companies, a UIT has a stated date for termination that varies according to the investments held in its portfolio. At termination, investors receive their proportionate share of the UIT net assets. For statistical information on UITs, see page 101.

An **exchange-traded fund** (ETF) is an investment company whose shares are traded intraday on stock exchanges at market-determined prices. Those ETFs currently in operation mirror stock indexes. Investors buy or sell ETF shares through a broker just as they would the shares of any publicly traded company. For statistical information on ETFs, see pages 102–103.

At the end of 2001, 8,307 mutual funds were available to investors, offering a wide variety of investment objectives, from conservative to aggressive, and exposure to a wide range of securities. The Investment Company Institute classifies mutual funds in 33 investment objective categories (see pages 8–11).

Liquidity

Since mutual funds are required by law to redeem shares on a daily basis, fund shares are a very liquid investment. Most mutual funds also continually offer new shares to investors, and many fund companies allow shareholders to transfer money—or make "exchanges"—from one fund to another within the same fund family. Mutual funds process sales, redemptions, and exchanges as a normal part of daily business activity.

The price per share at which shares are redeemed is known as the net asset value (NAV). NAV is the current market value of all the fund's assets, minus liabilities, divided by the total number of outstanding shares (see illustration below).

The price at which a fund's shares may be purchased is its NAV per share plus any applicable front-end sales charge (the offering price of a fund without a sales charge would be the same as its NAV per share).

How a Mutual Fund Determines Its Share Price

Mutual Fund X owns a portfolio of stocks worth $6 million dollars; its liabilities are $60,000; its shareholders own 500,000 shares.

$$\text{Fund Share Price or Net Asset Value (NAV)} \ \$11.88 \ = \ \frac{\text{Market Value in Dollars of a Fund's Securities Minus Its Liabilities (\$6,000,000 - \$60,000)}}{\text{Number of Investor Shares Outstanding (500,000)}}$$

Fund share prices appear in the financial pages of most major newspapers. A fund's share price can also be found in its semiannual and annual reports.

Mutual Fund Investment Objectives

The Investment Company Institute classifies U.S. mutual funds in 33 investment objective categories.

EQUITY FUNDS

Capital Appreciation Funds seek capital appreciation; dividends are not a primary consideration.

- *Aggressive growth funds* invest primarily in common stocks of small, growth companies.
- *Growth funds* invest primarily in common stocks of well-established companies.
- *Sector funds* invest primarily in companies in related fields.

Total Return Funds seek a combination of current income and capital appreciation.

- *Growth-and-income funds* invest primarily in common stocks of established companies with the potential for growth and a consistent record of dividend payments.
- *Income-equity funds* invest primarily in equity securities of companies with a consistent record of dividend payments. They seek income more than capital appreciation.

World Equity Funds invest primarily in stocks of foreign companies.

- *Emerging market funds* invest primarily in companies based in developing regions of the world.
- *Global equity funds* invest primarily in equity securities traded worldwide, including those of U.S. companies.
- *International equity funds* invest primarily in equity securities of companies located outside the United States.
- *Regional equity funds* invest in companies based in a specific part of the world.

HYBRID FUNDS

Hybrid Funds may invest in a mix of equities, fixed-income securities, and derivative instruments.

- *Asset allocation funds* invest in various asset classes including, but not limited to, equities, fixed-income securities, and money market instruments. They seek high total return by maintaining precise weightings in asset classes. Global asset allocation funds invest in a mix of equity and debt securities issued worldwide.
- *Balanced funds* invest in a mix of equity securities and bonds with the three-part objective of conserving principal, providing income, and achieving long-term growth of both principal and income. These funds maintain target percentages in asset classes.

- *Flexible portfolio funds* invest in common stocks, bonds, other debt securities, and money market securities to provide high total return. These funds may invest up to 100 percent in any one type of security and may easily change weightings depending upon market conditions.

- *Income-mixed funds* invest in a variety of income-producing securities, including equities and fixed-income instruments. These funds seek a high level of current income without regard to capital appreciation.

TAXABLE BOND FUNDS

Corporate Bond Funds seek current income by investing in high-quality debt securities issued by U.S. corporations.

- *Corporate bond funds—general* invest two-thirds or more of their portfolios in U.S. corporate bonds with no explicit restrictions on average maturity.

- *Corporate bond funds—intermediate-term* invest two-thirds or more of their portfolios in U.S. corporate bonds with an average maturity of five to 10 years. These funds seek a high level of income with less price volatility than longer-term bond funds.

- *Corporate bond funds—short-term* invest two-thirds or more of their portfolios in U.S. corporate bonds with an average maturity of one to five years. These funds seek a high level of income with less price volatility than intermediate-term bond funds.

High-Yield Funds invest two-thirds or more of their portfolios in lower-rated U.S. corporate bonds (Baa or lower by Moody's and BBB or lower by Standard and Poor's rating services).

World Bond Funds invest in debt securities offered by foreign companies and governments. They seek the highest level of current income available worldwide.

- *Global bond funds—general* invest in worldwide debt securities with no stated average maturity or an average maturity of five years or more. These funds may invest up to 25 percent of assets in companies located in the United States.

- *Global bond funds—short-term* invest in debt securities worldwide with an average maturity of one to five years. These funds may invest up to 25 percent of assets in companies located in the United States.

- *Other world bond funds*, such as international bond and emerging market debt funds, invest in foreign government and corporate debt instruments. Two-thirds of an international bond fund's portfolio must be invested outside the United States. Emerging market debt funds invest primarily in debt from underdeveloped regions of the world.

continued on page 10

continued from page 9

Government Bond Funds invest in U.S. government bonds of varying maturities. They seek high current income.

- *Government bond funds—general* invest two-thirds or more of their portfolios in U.S. government securities of no stated average maturity. Securities utilized by investment managers may change with market conditions.

- *Government bond funds—intermediate-term* invest two-thirds or more of their portfolios in U.S. government securities with an average maturity of five to 10 years. Securities utilized by investment managers may change with market conditions.

- *Government bond funds—short-term* invest two-thirds or more of their portfolios in U.S. government securities with an average maturity of one to five years. Securities utilized by investment managers may change with market conditions.

- *Mortgage-backed funds* invest two-thirds or more of their portfolios in pooled mortgage-backed securities.

Strategic Income Funds invest in a combination of U.S. fixed-income securities to provide a high level of current income.

TAX-FREE BOND FUNDS

State Municipal Bond Funds invest primarily in municipal bonds issued by a particular state. These funds seek high after-tax income for residents of individual states.

- *State municipal bond funds—general* invest primarily in single-state municipal bonds with an average maturity of greater than five years or no specific stated maturity. The income from these funds is largely exempt from federal as well as state income tax for residents of the state.

- *State municipal bond funds—short-term* invest primarily in single-state municipal bonds with an average maturity of one to five years. The income of these funds is largely exempt from federal as well as state income tax for residents of the state.

National Municipal Bond Funds invest primarily in the bonds of various municipal issuers in the United States. These funds seek high current income free from federal tax.

- *National municipal bond funds—general* invest primarily in municipal bonds with an average maturity of more than five years or no specific stated maturity.

- *National municipal bond funds—short-term* invest primarily in municipal bonds with an average maturity of one to five years.

MONEY MARKET FUNDS

Taxable Money Market Funds invest in short-term, high-grade money market securities and must have average maturities of 90 days or less. These funds seek the highest level of income consistent with preservation of capital (i.e., maintaining a stable share price).

- *Taxable money market funds—government* invest primarily in U.S. Treasury obligations and other financial instruments issued or guaranteed by the U.S. government, its agencies, or its instrumentalities.

- *Taxable money market funds—nongovernment* invest primarily in a variety of money market instruments, including certificates of deposit from large banks, commercial paper, and bankers acceptances.

Tax-Exempt Money Market Funds invest in short-term municipal securities and must have average maturities of 90 days or less. These funds seek the highest level of income—free from federal and, in some cases, state and local taxes—consistent with preservation of capital.

- *National tax-exempt money market funds* invest in short-term securities of various U.S. municipal issuers.

- *State tax-exempt money market funds* invest primarily in short-term securities of municipal issuers in a single state to achieve the highest level of tax-free income for residents of that state.

The Mutual Fund Pricing Process

Mutual fund pricing is an intensive process that takes place in a short time frame at the end of each business day. Generally, a fund's pricing process begins at the close of the New York Stock Exchange, normally 4:00 pm Eastern time. A mutual fund typically obtains the prices for securities it holds from a pricing service, a company that collects prices on a wide variety of securities. Fund accounting agents internally validate the prices received by subjecting them to various control procedures. In some instances, a fund may use more than one pricing service to ensure accuracy.

The vast majority of mutual funds release their daily share prices through Nasdaq. For a fund's share price to be published in the next day's morning newspapers, it must be delivered by 5:55 pm Eastern time to Nasdaq. As prices are received by Nasdaq, they are instantaneously transmitted to wire services and other subscribers. Wire services transmit the prices to their client newspapers. Besides in newspapers, daily fund prices are available from other sources. Many funds offer toll-free telephone service and Internet access, which provides the fund share prices along with other current information.

The NAV must reflect the current market value of the fund's securities, as long as market quotations for those securities are readily available. Other assets are priced at fair value, determined in good faith by a fund's board of directors. The Investment Company Act of 1940 requires "forward pricing": shareholders purchasing or redeeming shares receive the next computed share price following the fund's receipt of the transaction order.

Any income and expenses (including any fees) must be accrued through the date the share price is calculated. Changes in holdings and in the number of shares must be reflected no later than the first calculation of the share price on the next business day.

Funds typically value exchange-traded securities using the closing prices from the exchange on which the securities are principally traded, even if the exchange closes before the fund's daily pricing time (which occurs with many foreign securities). If a material event that will likely affect the value of a security occurs after the exchange closed and before the fund's share price is determined, it may be necessary to determine the fair value of the security in light of that event.

Accessibility

Mutual fund shares are available through a variety of sources. Investors outside retirement plans may purchase fund shares either with the help of an investment professional, such as a broker, financial planner, bank representative, or insurance agent, or directly from the fund itself, based on the investor's own research and knowledge. Investment professionals provide services to investors—analyzing the investors' financial needs and objectives and recommending appropriate funds. Investment professionals are compensated for their services, generally through a sales commission or through 12b-1 fees deducted from the fund's assets.

Many mutual funds can be purchased directly from fund companies without the help of an investment professional. When funds are purchased in this manner, investors are required to do their own research to determine which funds meet their needs.

Mutual funds may also be offered as investment selections in 401(k) plans and other employee benefit plans. See Chapter 5 for more information on mutual funds and the retirement market.

Mutual Fund Minimum Investment Requirements, 2001
(percent distribution of funds by minimum investment requirement)*

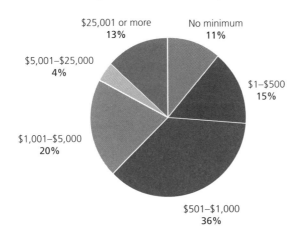

$25,001 or more
13%

No minimum
11%

$5,001–$25,000
4%

$1–$500
15%

$1,001–$5,000
20%

$501–$1,000
36%

*Many mutual funds offer lower investment minimums for Individual Retirement Accounts and automatic investment plans.

Note: Components do not sum to 100 percent due to rounding.

Shareholder Services

Mutual funds offer a wide variety of services to shareholders. These services include toll-free telephone service, 24-hour telephone access to account information and transaction processing, consolidated account statements, shareholder cost basis (tax) information, exchanges between funds, automatic investments, checkwriting privileges on money market and some bond funds, automatic reinvestment of fund dividends, and automatic withdrawals. Mutual funds also provide extensive investor education and other shareholder communications, including newsletters, brochures, retirement and other planning guides, and websites.

Affordability

Mutual funds offer their many benefits and services at an affordable price. Furthermore, competition within the fund industry helps keep funds affordable, as the results of studies by the SEC and the General Accounting Office show. For more information on the trends in mutual fund costs, see the ICI website at www.ici.org/newsroom/industry_issues_fees.html.

Mutual Fund Fees and Expenses

Mutual fund shareholders benefit from full disclosure of mutual fund fees and expenses. A fund's fees and expenses are required by law to be clearly disclosed to investors in a standardized fee table at the front of the fund's prospectus. The fee table breaks out the fees and expenses shareholders can expect to pay when purchasing fund shares and allows investors to easily compare the cost of investing in different funds.

SHAREHOLDER FEES

These fees are charged directly to an investor for a specific transaction, such as a purchase, redemption, or exchange.

- **Sales Charge.** A sales charge may be attached to the purchase or sale of mutual fund shares. This fee compensates a financial professional for his or her services.
- **Redemption Fee.** This fee is paid to a fund to cover the costs, other than sales costs, involved with a redemption.
- **Exchange Fee.** This fee may be charged when an investor transfers money from one fund to another within the same fund family.
- **Annual Account Maintenance Fee.** This fee may be charged by some funds, for example, to cover the costs of providing service to low-balance accounts.

ANNUAL FUND OPERATING EXPENSES

These fees and expenses reflect the normal costs of operating a fund. Unlike shareholder fees, these expenses are not charged directly to an investor but are deducted from fund assets before earnings are distributed to shareholders.

- **Management Fee.** This is a fee charged by a fund's investment adviser for managing the fund's portfolio of securities and providing related services.
- **Distribution (12b-1) Fee.** This fee, if charged, is deducted from fund assets to pay marketing and advertising expenses or, more commonly, to compensate sales professionals.
- **Other Expenses.** These expenses include, for example, fees paid to a fund's transfer agent for providing fund shareholder services, such as toll-free phone communications, computerized account services, website services, recordkeeping, printing, and mailing.

CHAPTER 2

Regulation and Taxation of Mutual Funds

Mutual funds and their principal service providers are regulated by the federal government to protect investors and maintain public confidence in the fund industry.

The U.S. Securities and Exchange Commission (SEC) regulates funds according to the provisions of the Investment Company Act of 1940. Funds must also comply with the Securities Act of 1933 when registering their shares publicly, and must provide notice filings to those states in which they intend to offer their shares. In addition, when fund sponsors sell fund shares to the public they are subject to regulation as broker-dealers under the Securities Exchange Act of 1934. Furthermore, fund investment advisers are generally required to register under the Investment Advisers Act of 1940.

The Foundation of Fund Regulation: The Investment Company Act of 1940

The Investment Company Act, enacted on August 23, 1940, set the structure and regulatory framework for the modern mutual fund industry. The 1940 Act has stood the test of time because of its wide-ranging provisions, which impose restrictions not only on mutual funds but also fund investment advisers, principal underwriters, directors, officers, and employees. Perhaps equally important, the 1940 Act grants the SEC broad discretionary powers to keep the Act current with the constantly changing financial service industry environment in which mutual funds and other investment companies operate.

Taxation, Tax Exemption, and Tax Deferral

Unlike most corporations, a mutual fund generally distributes all of its earnings each year and is taxed only on amounts it retains. This specialized "pass-through" tax treatment of mutual fund income and capital gains was established under the Revenue Act of 1936 and endures today under Subchapter M of the Internal Revenue Code of 1986. To qualify for this favorable tax treatment under the Code, mutual funds must meet, among other conditions, various investment diversification standards and pass a test regarding the source of their income.

Four Principal Securities Laws Govern Mutual Funds

The Investment Company Act of 1940 regulates the structure and operations of mutual funds and other investment companies. Among other things, the 1940 Act requires mutual funds to maintain detailed books and records, safeguard their portfolio securities, and file semiannual reports with the U.S. Securities and Exchange Commission (SEC).

The Securities Act of 1933 requires federal registration of all public offerings of securities, including mutual fund shares. The 1933 Act also requires that all prospective investors receive a current prospectus describing the fund.

The Securities Exchange Act of 1934 regulates broker-dealers, including mutual fund principal underwriters and others who sell mutual fund shares, and requires them to register with the SEC. Among other things, the 1934 Act requires registered broker-dealers to maintain extensive books and records, segregate customer securities in adequate custodial accounts, and file detailed, annual financial reports with the SEC.

The Investment Advisers Act of 1940 requires federal registration of all investment advisers to mutual funds. The Advisers Act contains various antifraud provisions and requires fund advisers to meet recordkeeping, reporting, and other requirements.

Fund investors are ultimately responsible for paying tax on a fund's earnings, whether or not they receive the distributions in cash or reinvest them in additional fund shares. As a result, the fund industry supports legislative efforts that would permit mutual fund shareholders to defer the tax on reinvested long-term capital gains distributions until shares are sold in order to reduce the tax burden on middle-income taxpayers while at the same time encouraging long-term investment in our economy.

Types of Distributions

Mutual funds make two types of taxable distributions to shareholders every year: ordinary dividends and capital gains. Dividend distributions come primarily from the interest and dividends earned by the securities in a fund's portfolio, after expenses are paid by the fund. These distributions must be reported as dividends on an investor's tax return. Capital gain distributions represent a fund's net gains, if any, from the sale of securities held in its portfolio for more than one year. When gains from these sales exceed losses, they are distributed to shareholders. Beginning in 2001, distributions of capital gains on assets held by the fund for more than five years were eligible for treatment as "qualified five-year gains"—taxable at an 8 percent rate—to those investors otherwise taxed on these gains at a 10 percent rate.

To help mutual fund shareholders understand the impact that taxes can have on the returns generated by their investments, the SEC adopted a rule that beginning in 2002 requires mutual funds to disclose standardized after-tax returns for one-, five-, and 10-year periods. After-tax returns, which accompany before-tax returns in fund prospectuses, are presented in two ways:

- after taxes on fund distributions only (pre-liquidation); and
- after taxes on fund distributions and an assumed redemption of fund shares (post-liquidation).

While understanding the tax consequences of investing in mutual funds is important, the assumptions in the after-tax return calculations do not necessarily reflect the current tax situation of every investor. For example, the new SEC rules require after-tax returns to be calculated using the highest individual federal income tax rate—a rate that applies only to a very small portion of fund shareholders. In addition, short-term capital gain rates are used in the one-year after-tax return post-liquidation calculation; however, holding shares for one more day would make them eligible for lower long-term capital gain rates.

Share Sales and Exchanges

An investor who sells mutual fund shares usually incurs a capital gain or loss in the year the shares are sold; an exchange of shares between funds in the same fund family also results in either a capital gain or loss (see *Tax-Deferred Retirement Accounts* on page 21 for exceptions to these rules).

Investors are liable for tax on any capital gain arising from the sale of fund shares, just as they would be if they sold a stock, bond, or any other security. Capital losses from mutual fund share sales and exchanges, like capital losses from other investments, may be used to offset other gains in the current year and thereafter.

The amount of a shareholder's gain or loss on fund shares is determined by the difference between the "cost basis" of the shares (generally, the purchase price for shares, including those acquired with reinvested dividends) and the sale price. Many funds provide cost basis information to shareholders or compute gains and losses for shares sold.

Tax-Exempt Funds

Tax-exempt bond funds pay dividends earned from municipal bond interest. This income is exempt from federal income tax and, in some cases, state and local taxes as well. Tax-exempt money market funds invest in short-term municipal securities and also pay exempt-interest dividends.

Even though income from these two types of funds is generally tax-exempt, investors must report it on their income tax returns. Tax-exempt mutual funds provide investors with this information in a year-end statement, and they typically explain how to handle tax-exempt dividends on a state-by-state basis. For some taxpayers, portions of income earned by tax-exempt funds may also be subject to the federal alternative minimum tax.

Even though municipal bond dividends and interest may be tax-free, an investor who redeems tax-exempt fund shares may realize a taxable capital gain. An investor may also realize a taxable gain from a tax-exempt fund if the fund manager sells securities during the year for a net gain.

Tax-Deferred Retirement Accounts

Mutual fund investments in certain retirement accounts are tax-deductible and, generally, dividend and capital gain distributions remaining in the accounts accrue tax-deferred until distributed from the account.

In employer-sponsored 401(k) plans, for example, individuals typically contribute pre-tax dollars from their salary to an account in the plan. Similarly, IRA contributions may be tax-deductible, depending upon a person's eligibility to participate in an employer-sponsored retirement plan and their adjusted gross income.

Taxes on mutual fund earnings are deferred when they remain in 401(k) plans, IRAs, and other similar tax-deferred accounts, such as 403(b) accounts. Thus, no tax is incurred as a result of dividend and capital gain distributions, or from the sale of fund shares, until the investor takes distributions from the tax-deferred account.

Distributions are treated as income, which is subject to the investor's federal income tax rate at the time of distribution. (Nondeductible or after-tax contributions to these retirement accounts are not subject to taxation at distribution, and distributions from Roth IRAs also may not be subject to taxation at distribution.)

For most investors, distributions from tax-deferred accounts typically begin at or near retirement age, at which time the individual may be in a lower income tax bracket. Investors who receive proceeds from tax-deferred accounts prior to age 59½ may incur a tax penalty in addition to federal, state, and local income taxes.

CHAPTER 3

U.S. Mutual Fund Developments in 2001

U.S. households and businesses increased their reliance on mutual funds in 2001, and a record $505 billion net inflow of cash to funds offset the effects of falling stock prices to keep fund assets near $7 trillion for the second straight year.

All four major categories of mutual funds—equity, hybrid, bond, and money market—experienced net inflows in 2001, the first time in three years. Money market funds drew record inflows; bond and hybrid funds flows turned positive for the first year since 1998; and equity fund net new cash—while off previous years' high inflows—remained positive despite prolonged weakness in the stock markets.

Assets of Mutual Funds, 1990–2001
(trillions of dollars)

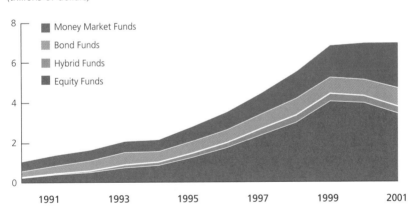

Note: See page 105 for data points on this chart.

Components of Mutual Fund Asset Growth,* 1990–2001
(trillions of dollars)

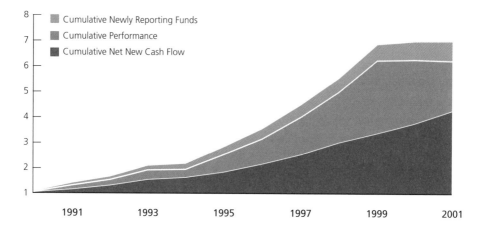

All total asset figures plotted in this chart represent the cumulative contribution of newly reporting funds, net new cash flow, and fund investment performance from year-end 1989 through the end of each year plotted. Asset levels plotted also include year-end 1989 assets of $981 billion.

Note: See page 106 for data points on this chart.

Household Demand for Mutual Funds

As in prior years, U.S. households remain net buyers of stocks and bonds through mutual funds and net sellers of these securities through other means. In 2001, mutual funds purchased an estimated $120 billion of stocks on behalf of U.S. households, while households sold an estimated $295 billion of stocks held outside mutual funds. Funds also acquired an estimated $130 billion of bonds for households, while households sold an estimated $132 billion of bonds held directly or through other means.

Meanwhile, the number of U.S. households owning mutual funds reached 54.8 million as of May 2001, up from 51.7 million in May 2000. As a result, more than half of the estimated 105.5 million U.S. households now own mutual funds, and an estimated 93.3 million individual shareholders in those households invest in funds—up from 89.7 million in May 2000.

Net New Cash Flow to Mutual Funds, 1990–2001
(billions of dollars)

	Equity	Hybrid	Bond	Money Market	Total*	Total Mutual Fund Assets
1990	$12.9	$1.5	$6.8	$23.2	$44.4	$1,065.2
1991	39.9	7.1	59.2	5.5	111.7	1,393.2
1992	79.0	21.8	70.9	(16.3)	155.4	1,642.5
1993	127.3	44.2	70.6	(14.1)	227.9	2,070.0
1994	114.5	23.1	(62.5)	8.8	83.9	2,155.3
1995	124.4	3.9	(6.1)	89.4	211.6	2,811.3
1996	216.9	12.2	2.8	89.4	321.3	3,525.8
1997	227.1	16.5	28.4	102.1	374.1	4,468.2
1998	157.0	10.2	74.6	235.3	477.1	5,525.2
1999	187.7	(13.8)	(4.1)	193.6	363.4	6,846.3
2000	309.4	(30.7)	(49.8)	159.6	388.5	6,964.7
2001	31.9	9.5	87.7	375.6	504.8	6,975.0

Components may not sum to the total due to rounding.

Net Purchases of Stocks and Bonds by Households, 1990–2001
(billions of dollars)

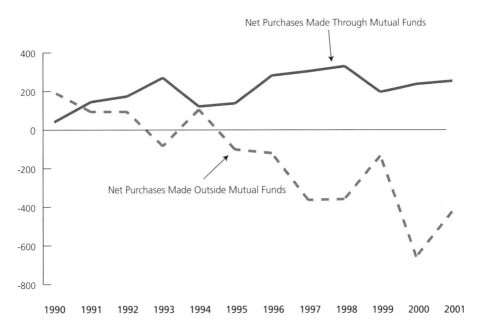

Net Purchases Made Through Mutual Funds

Net Purchases Made Outside Mutual Funds

Note: See page 107 for data points on this chart.

Sources: Federal Reserve Board and Investment Company Institute

Equity Funds

Since most U.S. mutual fund shareholders invest in funds as a means to achieve long-term objectives like planning for retirement and education saving (see *The Retirement and Education Savings Markets,* on page 45), equity funds continue to compose a large portion of overall fund industry assets—49 percent by year-end 2001. Yet even with households' continued affinity for equity funds, mutual funds still held only about 21 percent of all publicly traded U.S. equity by year-end 2001. Pension funds, insurance companies, and households' direct holdings accounted for the great majority, 79 percent.

Amid the dim economic and market conditions in 2001, equity mutual fund assets fell to $3.418 trillion, down from $3.962 trillion 12 months earlier. The lower asset figures were entirely the result of the declining value of the stocks held in equity funds. Net new cash flow, while still positive in 2001, declined to $32 billion from $309 billion in 2000.

Despite the declining value of investors' equity fund portfolios, however, the 2001 share of household equity assets held in mutual funds remains high, at 32 percent, up from 9 percent in 1990.

Mutual Fund Ownership of U.S. Corporate Equity
(percent)

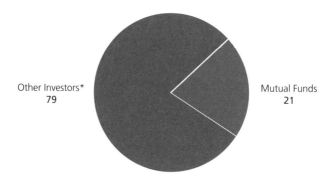

Other Investors*
79

Mutual Funds
21

Value of Publicly Held U.S. Equity Outstanding: $13.9 trillion
December 31, 2001

*Other investors include U.S. households, pension funds, and insurance companies.

Sources: Investment Company Institute, Nasdaq, AMEX, and NYSE

Net New Cash Flow to U.S. Equity Funds, Domestic vs. Foreign, 1990–2001
(billions of dollars)

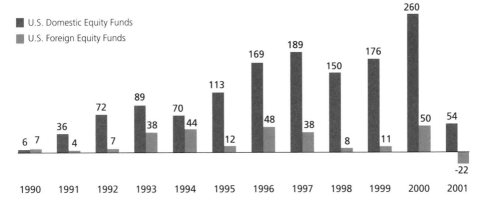

■ U.S. Domestic Equity Funds
▨ U.S. Foreign Equity Funds

Note: The sum of the net flows to foreign and domestic funds may not equal the totals shown on page 25 because of rounding. Data for funds that invest in other mutual funds were excluded from the series.

U.S. Domestic Equity Funds

U.S. domestic equity fund shareholder transaction activity the past two years resembled that observed during past bear markets. Monthly sales and redemptions moved lower over the course of 2000 and 2001. Sales declined more than redemptions, leading to weaker net new cash flow. The reaction of domestic equity fund shareholders to September 11 was muted. The pace of outflows had picked up in late summer, and quickened somewhat after September 11.

The persistence of the 2000–01 bear market and the downturn in September 2001 eroded domestic equity fund asset values. At the low point in September, domestic equity fund assets fell to $2.6 trillion, down 23 percent from the end of 2000 and off 31 percent from the stock market peak in March 2000. Domestic equity fund assets rose with stock prices through the remainder of 2001 and by the end of December reached $3.0 trillion. Net new cash flow slowed to $54 billion in 2001, down from $260 billion in 2000. The slowdown of net inflow in 2001 was concentrated in funds with growth-oriented objectives.

U.S. Foreign Equity Funds

Assets in U.S. mutual funds that primarily invest in companies outside the U.S. declined by 21 percent in 2001 to $429 billion. These funds experienced outflows totaling $22 billion in 2001.

The weaker demand for U.S. foreign equity funds continued a pattern begun in 2000, when foreign equity markets moved lower with U.S. markets and when many foreign currencies declined relative to the U.S. dollar. Falling equity prices abroad and a further depreciation of foreign currencies in 2001 held down the performance of foreign equity funds. The reaction of investors in foreign equity funds to September 11 was muted.

Bond and Hybrid Funds

Bond funds added $88 billion in net new cash in 2001, the highest inflow since 1986. Bond fund assets rose to $925 billion at year-end 2001. Hybrid funds posted a net inflow of $10 billion, and assets in these funds were relatively unchanged at $346 billion.

The stronger demand for bond funds reflected typical shareholder response to declining interest rates. Yields on medium-term U.S. Treasury and other highly rated debt instruments fell during most of the year, and returns on bond funds holding these securities rose, boosting demand for these funds. September 11 events had little effect on investor flows to bond funds. Inflows were strong in the late summer and were concentrated in funds investing in U.S. Treasury and agency debt securities. Flows remained robust in the wake of the attacks and were largely directed toward the same types of bond funds.

Inflows to hybrid funds occurred despite negative returns. Hybrid fund flows, like bond fund flows, are heavily influenced by interest rates. As interest rates declined in 2000 and 2001, outflows from hybrid funds turned to inflows. Hybrid funds experienced outflows in early 2000 following a period of rising interest rates. As rates began to fall in 2000, outflows slowed. Rates continued to decline in 2001 and hybrid funds experienced sustained inflows for the first time since 1998.

Net New Cash Flow to Bond and Hybrid Funds, 1990–2001
(billions of dollars)

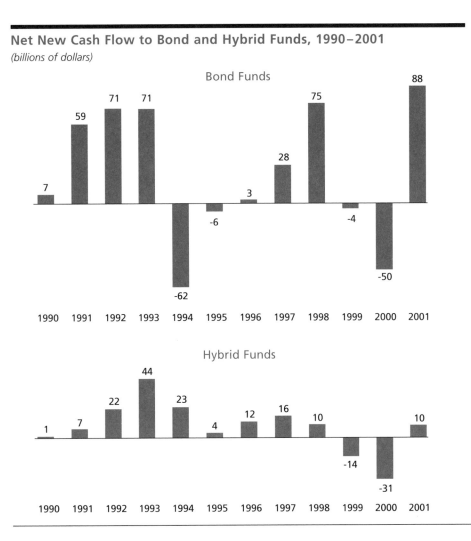

Bond Funds

1990	1991	1992	1993	1994	1995	1996	1997	1998	1999	2000	2001
7	59	71	71	-62	-6	3	28	75	-4	-50	88

Hybrid Funds

1990	1991	1992	1993	1994	1995	1996	1997	1998	1999	2000	2001
1	7	22	44	23	4	12	16	10	-14	-31	10

Money Market Funds

Money market fund assets accounted for one-third of all mutual fund assets by year-end 2001, the highest share of industry assets in these funds since 1992. Investors—particularly institutional investors—put a record $376 billion in money funds during the year, and money fund assets reached an all-time high of $2.285 trillion.

Inflows to retail money funds slowed to $37 billion in 2001 from $43 billion in 2000, as yields on these funds fell relative to savings deposit rates. However, institutional money funds attracted $339 billion for the year—nearly three times more than in 2000—as open market short-term interest

Share of U.S. Nonfinancial Business Short-Term Assets* Held Through Money Market Funds, 1990–2001

(percent of total)

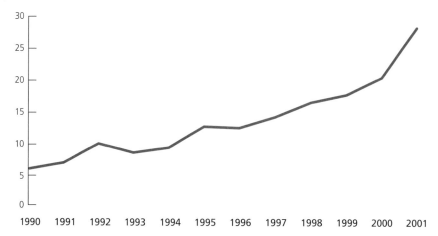

*Business short-term assets consist of foreign deposits, checkable deposits, time and savings deposits, money market funds, repurchase agreements, and commercial paper.

Note: See page 108 for data points on this chart.

Sources: Federal Reserve Board and Investment Company Institute

rates were below money market yields intermittently throughout the year. Businesses and other institutional investors responded to the yield advantage on institutional money funds by shifting short-term assets into money market mutual funds.

The movement of short-term assets into mutual funds continues the increasing trend of businesses to turn to money market funds for cash management during the 1990s. Money fund assets held by businesses— excluding financial services companies—grew at an annual rate of 27 percent between 1990 and 2001, increasing from $26 billion to $350 billion. As a result of this growth, money funds' share of short-term business assets rose from 6 percent in 1990 to 28 percent in 2001.

The growth in business holdings of money funds is partly due to corporations' preference to outsource cash management to mutual funds rather than holding liquid securities directly. By using money funds, these corporations benefit from economies of scale provided by mutual funds that they would be unable to achieve through internal management of their liquid assets.

Net New Cash Flow to Money Market Funds, Retail vs. Institutional, 1990–2001

(billions of dollars)

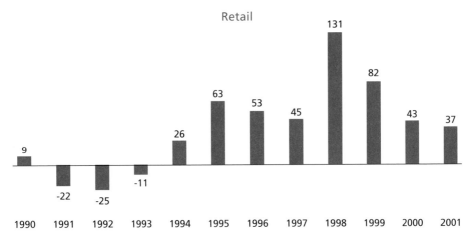

Retail

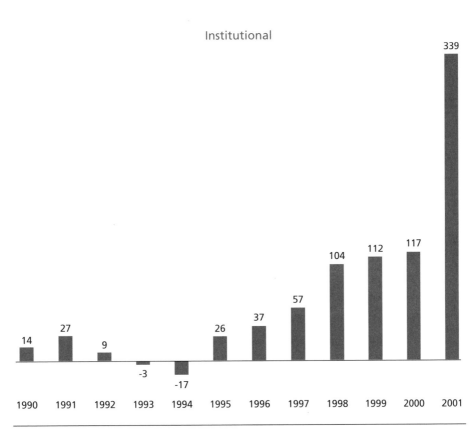

Institutional

Capital Gain Distributions Paid by Mutual Funds, 1996–2001
(billions of dollars)

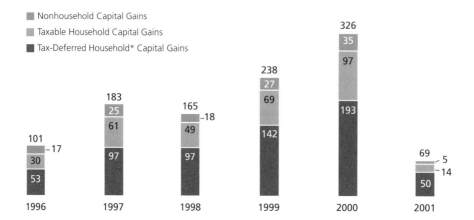

- Nonhousehold Capital Gains
- Taxable Household Capital Gains
- Tax-Deferred Household* Capital Gains

*Households are defined to exclude mutual fund assets attributed to business corporations, financial institutions, nonprofit organizations, other institutional investors, and fiduciaries.

Note: Components may not sum to total because of rounding.

Other 2001 Industry Developments

Capital Gain Distributions Decline

Mutual funds distributed an estimated $69 billion in capital gains to shareholders in 2001, the lowest level since 1995 and significantly less than the $326 billion distributed in 2000.

The smaller capital gain distributions in 2001 occurred because falling equity prices reduced the unrealized appreciation that many funds built up in the late 1990s. Most gains are paid from equity funds, and unrealized gains in these funds had grown to an estimated $1.5 trillion at the end of 1999, or nearly 40 percent of equity fund assets. By September 2001, these gains had been paid out or eliminated by falling stock prices, and unrealized losses in equity funds totaled an estimated $300 billion or 10 percent of equity fund assets.

Equity and hybrid funds accounted for 96 percent of the $69 billion of the capital gain distributed to shareholders in 2001, and more than three-quarters of all capital gain distributions paid to households were estimated to have been paid to tax-deferred accounts, such as IRAs, defined contribution plans, and variable annuities.

Distribution Channel Sources Shift

With the rising demand for mutual funds in the 1990s, fund companies and distribution companies developed new outlets for selling mutual funds and expanded traditional sales channels. Overall, the estimated share of new long-term fund sales made directly to retail investors decreased from 23 percent in 1990 to 15 percent in 2001. Meanwhile, the new sales of long-term funds made to retail investors through third parties or to institutional investors rose from 77 percent to 85 percent.

Many fund complexes that primarily market directly to investors have turned increasingly to third parties and intermediaries for distribution. (Third-party distribution channels include employer-sponsored pension plans, mutual fund supermarkets, fee-based advisors, mutual fund wrap account programs, and bank trust departments.) For example, in 1990, an estimated 64 percent of new sales of direct-marketed funds were direct sales to retail investors, such as via mail, by telephone or the Internet, or at office locations; by year-end 2001, this share had fallen to 37 percent. Meanwhile, the share of new sales of direct-marketed funds conducted through third-parties or to institutional investors increased from 36 percent to 63 percent.

Share of New Sales of Long-Term Funds by Distribution Channel, Selected Years
(percent)

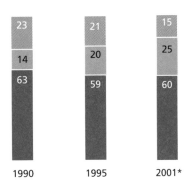

- Direct Sales to Retail Investors
- Third-Party and Institutional Sales–Direct Market
- Third-Party and Institutional Sales–Sales Force

	1990	1995	2001*
Direct Sales to Retail Investors	23	21	15
Third-Party and Institutional Sales–Direct Market	14	20	25
Third-Party and Institutional Sales–Sales Force	63	59	60

Preliminary data

Number of Mutual Funds, 1990–2001

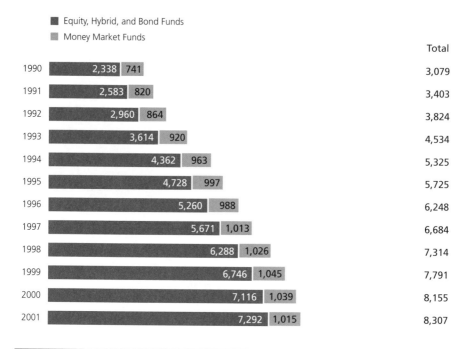

- ■ Equity, Hybrid, and Bond Funds
- ■ Money Market Funds

Year	Equity, Hybrid, and Bond Funds	Money Market Funds	Total
1990	2,338	741	3,079
1991	2,583	820	3,403
1992	2,960	864	3,824
1993	3,614	920	4,534
1994	4,362	963	5,325
1995	4,728	997	5,725
1996	5,260	988	6,248
1997	5,671	1,013	6,684
1998	6,288	1,026	7,314
1999	6,746	1,045	7,791
2000	7,116	1,039	8,155
2001	7,292	1,015	8,307

Likewise, funds that were traditionally sold through a sales force of brokers shifted increasingly to nontraditional sources of sales such as employer-sponsored pension plans, banks, and life insurance companies in the 1990s. By year-end 2001, the share of new sales of sales-force funds through nontraditional sources rose to 46 percent from 25 percent in 1990.

New Funds Grow at Reduced Pace and Industry Concentration Reverses

The number of mutual funds grew by just 152 in 2001, the smallest increase since 1981. The slowdown in net fund formation reflects several forces. First, the bear market in stocks during 2000 and 2001 dampened the formation of new equity funds. In addition, fund complexes have been merging and liquidating municipal bond funds since the mid-1990s when inflows to these funds began to slacken from the pace set earlier in the decade.

Fund sponsors that were involved in mergers in the past few years have also streamlined their product offerings and combined funds with overlapping investment objectives. In 2001, there were 373 mergers of mutual funds. Roughly half of these mergers were between two funds of formerly separate sponsors that had been involved in a merger or acquisition in the past decade.

The mergers and acquisitions of recent years have not increased the concentration of industry assets among the largest mutual fund complexes. Indeed, the concentration of assets among the five and 10 largest complexes has declined slightly in the past few years. The five largest sponsors managed one-third of the industry's assets in 2001, down from 35 percent in 1999. Assets managed by the 10 largest firms fell to 46 percent of the industry's assets from 50 percent in 1999. Some of the drop is explained by the relative performance of different asset classes. The largest firms hold a greater portion of the assets that they manage in equity funds, which have underperformed bond and money market funds for the past two years. Assets of these fund sponsors have shrunk in size relative to those firms having a larger share of their business in fixed-income funds.

Share of Assets at Largest Mutual Fund Complexes,* Selected Years
(percent of industry total)

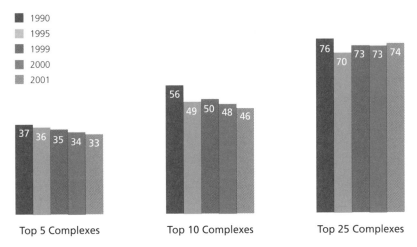

■ 1990
▒ 1995
■ 1999
■ 2000
■ 2001

Top 5 Complexes: 37 36 35 34 33

Top 10 Complexes: 56 49 50 48 46

Top 25 Complexes: 76 70 73 73 74

Variable annuities are excluded from the calculation of concentration ratios.

CHAPTER 4

Mutual Fund Ownership and Shareholder Characteristics

An estimated 93.3 million individuals in 54.8 million U.S. households owned the majority of the mutual fund industry's $6.975 trillion in assets at year-end 2001. Individuals held 76 percent of mutual fund assets, while fiduciaries—banks and individuals serving as trustees, guardians, or administrators—and other institutional investors held the remaining 24 percent.

Mutual Fund Assets by Type of Owner, 1991 and 2001
(percent of total mutual fund assets)

■ Financial, business, and other organizations
▨ Fiduciaries
▨ U.S. households[1]

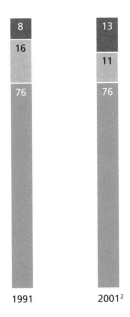

1991   2001[2]

[1]*Household holdings include mutual funds held in retail accounts as well as through employer-sponsored pension plans, individual retirement accounts, and variable annuities.*

[2]*Preliminary data*

Note: Total assets of mutual funds were $1.393 trillion at year-end 1991 and $6.975 trillion at year-end 2001.

U.S. Household Financial Assets

U.S. households own many financial assets, including mutual funds, stocks, bonds, and bank deposits. In 2001, households made $478 billion of net purchases of financial assets, up from $312 billion in 2000. On balance, households were net sellers of directly held stocks and bonds but net buyers of mutual funds.

U.S. households invested $275 billion of their total net purchases of financial assets in mutual funds (including reinvested dividends) in 2001. Long-term mutual funds—equity, hybrid, and bond funds—accounted for $190 billion and money market funds, $85 billion.

U.S. Household Ownership of Mutual Funds, 1980–2001*
(percent of all U.S. households)

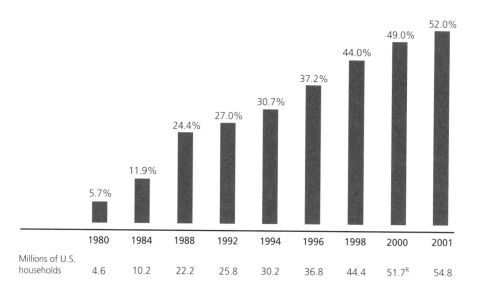

	1980	1984	1988	1992	1994	1996	1998	2000	2001
	5.7%	11.9%	24.4%	27.0%	30.7%	37.2%	44.0%	49.0%	52.0%
Millions of U.S. households	4.6	10.2	22.2	25.8	30.2	36.8	44.4	51.7ᴿ	54.8

*Households owning mutual funds in 1980 and 1984 were estimated from data on the number of accounts held by individual shareholders and the number of funds owned by fund-owning households; data for 1980 through 1992 exclude households owning mutual funds only through employer-sponsored retirement plans; data for 1994 through 2001 include households owning mutual funds only through employer-sponsored retirement plans. The data for 1998 through 2001 include fund ownership through variable annuities.

R = Revised

U.S. Shareholder Characteristics

In 2001, the typical mutual fund investor was middle-aged, married, and saving for retirement. More specifically, the typical fund investor was 46 years old, with median household income of $62,100, median household financial assets of $100,000, and household mutual fund assets of $40,000.

More than two-thirds of households with mutual fund holdings were headed by individuals in the primary income-earning years from age 35 to 64. Only 19 percent of shareholders were retired from their primary occupations.

Fund Shareholders Demonstrate a Long-Term Perspective

Most shareholders invest in funds for retirement, are willing to take at least moderate risk for moderate gain, and are not focused on short-term market fluctuations.

More than 80 percent of all mutual fund-owning households participate in employer-sponsored defined contribution retirement plans. Sixty-two percent of fund-owning households own mutual funds in their defined contribution plans, and nearly half view the workplace as their primary purchase channel for mutual funds. Sixty percent have Individual Retirement Accounts.

Nearly nine out of 10 fund households include equity funds among their holdings. On average, equity fund investments represent 65 percent of shareholders' mutual fund portfolios. Seventy-eight percent of mutual fund shareholders are employed full- or part-time. In married households, the spouse also tends to work. Nearly half of all household fund owners made their first mutual fund purchase before 1990, and 39 percent bought their first fund between 1990 and 1997.

Investment decisionmaking is shared in 53 percent of fund-owning households. Males are the sole decisionmakers in 24 percent of fund-

U.S. Mutual Fund Shareholder Characteristics[1]

Median

Age[2]	46 years
Household income	$62,100
Household financial assets[3]	$100,000
Household mutual fund assets	$40,000
Number of mutual funds owned	4

Percent

Household investment decisionmaker:	
Male is sole decisionmaker	24
Female is sole decisionmaker	23
Co-decisionmakers	53
Married or living with a partner[2]	67
Four-year college degree or more[2]	52
Employed[2]	78
Spouse or partner employed[4]	77
Own:[5]	
Equity funds	88
Bond funds	37
Hybrid funds	34
Money market funds	48
Own mutual funds bought:[5]	
Outside defined contribution retirement plan(s) (total)	69
Sales force[6]	55
Direct market[7]	33
Inside defined contribution retirement plan(s) (total)	62
Primary mutual fund purchase channel:	
Outside defined contribution retirement plan(s) (total)	52
Sales force[6]	37
Direct market[7]	15
Inside defined contribution retirement plan(s)	48

[1]As of 2001.

[2]Refers to the household's responding financial decisionmaker for mutual fund investments.

[3]Excludes primary residence but includes assets in employer-sponsored retirement plans.

[4]Percent of shareholders married or living with a partner.

[5]Multiple responses included.

[6]Includes funds purchased from full-service brokers, insurance agents, financial planners, and bank representatives.

[7]Includes funds purchased directly from fund companies and through discount brokers.

Note: Number of respondents varies.

owning households, females in 23 percent. Members of the Baby Boom Generation (individuals born between 1946 and 1964) make up the greatest percentage of mutual fund shareholders, at 52 percent. Twenty-five percent of fund shareholders are members of the so-called Silent Generation (born before 1946), and 23 percent are members of Generation X (born in 1965 or later). Thirty percent of mutual fund shareholders reside in the South; 26 percent in the Midwest; 25 percent in the West; and 19 percent in the Northeast.

Shareholders' Use of the Internet

Approximately eight in 10 U.S. households owning mutual funds used the Internet between June 2000 and May 2001, up from 68 percent between April 1999 and March 2000.

Although shareholders' use of the Internet has increased, most continue to use non-Internet methods to invest in fund shares and redeem them. Twenty-four percent of all shareholders who conducted equity mutual fund transactions between June 2000 and May 2001 bought or sold equity fund

---

Mutual Fund Shareholders' Use of the Internet, 2001*
(percent of households owning mutual funds)

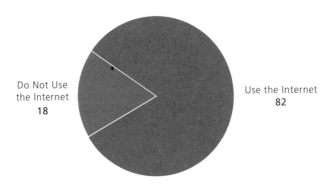

Do Not Use the Internet
18

Use the Internet
82

---

*In the 12 months preceding the survey (June 2000 through May 2001). Excludes shareholders using the Internet only to send or receive e-mail.

shares online. Slightly more than half of this group purchased equity fund shares only, about a third both bought and sold equity fund shares, and 15 percent sold equity fund shares only.

These shareholders conducted a median of two equity fund transactions over the Internet and an average of eight between June 2000 and May 2001, indicating that a small number of shareholders conducted a high volume of online equity fund transactions.

Shareholders who used the Internet to conduct equity fund transactions were generally younger and had greater household income and financial assets than shareholders who did not use the Internet when making equity fund transactions. The median age of online shareholders who used the Internet to conduct equity fund transactions was 43. This group had median household income of $87,500 and median household financial assets of $200,000. Online shareholders conducting equity fund transactions typically had $87,500 invested in seven mutual funds. Shareholders who did not use the Internet to make equity fund transactions were typically 45 years old, had median household income of $65,700 and financial assets of $125,000. These shareholders had a median of $55,000 invested in five mutual funds.

Use of the Internet to Conduct Equity Mutual Fund Transactions, 2001

Equity Mutual Fund Transaction Activity*

(percent of U.S. households owning mutual funds)

Method Used to Conduct Equity Mutual Fund Transactions*

(percent of U.S. households owning mutual funds that conducted an equity mutual fund transaction)

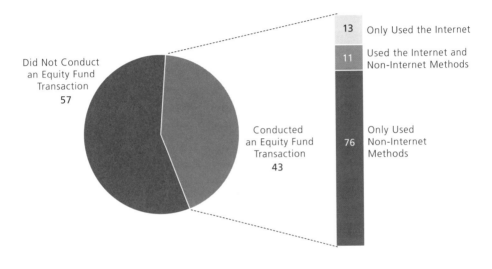

Did Not Conduct
an Equity Fund
Transaction
57

Conducted
an Equity Fund
Transaction
43

13   Only Used the Internet

11   Used the Internet and
Non-Internet Methods

76   Only Used
Non-Internet
Methods

*In the 12 months preceding the survey (June 2000 through May 2001).

CHAPTER 5

Retirement and Education Savings Markets

Saving for retirement and education are important investment objectives, and many Americans use mutual funds to reach these goals.

At year-end 2001, mutual funds accounted for $2.4 trillion, or 22 percent, of the $10.9 trillion U.S. retirement market. The remaining $8.6 trillion of 2001 retirement market assets were managed by pension funds, insurance companies, banks, and brokerage firms. In the emerging education savings market, mutual funds accounted for an estimated 98 percent of the $8.5 billion Section 529 savings plan market at year-end 2001. Funds also managed $2 billion in Coverdell Education Savings Account— formerly Education IRA—assets by year-end.

U.S. Retirement Market Assets, 2001[1,2]

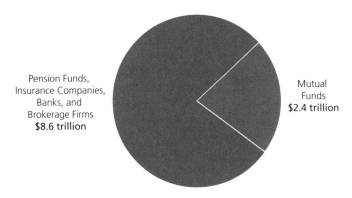

Pension Funds,
Insurance Companies,
Banks, and
Brokerage Firms
$8.6 trillion

Mutual
Funds
$2.4 trillion

Total: $10.9 trillion

[1]*Preliminary data*

[2]*Components do not sum to total U.S. retirement market assets due to rounding.*

Sources: Investment Company Institute and Federal Reserve Board

Mutual Fund Retirement Assets, 1991–2001[1]

(billions of dollars)

	Total Retirement	Employer-Sponsored Accounts[2]	IRAs
1991	$335	$147	$188
1992	437	199	237
1993	608	285	322
1994	687	337	350
1995	940	464	476
1996	1,195	598	597
1997	1,559	783	776
1998	1,963	990	974
1999	2,547	1,284	1,263
2000	2,476	1,240	1,236
2001	2,356	1,189	1,168

[1]Preliminary data

[2]Includes private defined contribution plans (401(k), 403(b), 457, and others), state and local government employee retirement funds, and private defined benefit plans.

Note: Components may not add to totals due to rounding.

Sources: Investment Company Institute, Federal Reserve Board, Internal Revenue Service, and Department of Labor

Retirement Accounts Hold About One-Third of Fund Assets

The $2.4 trillion in mutual fund retirement assets represented about one-third of all mutual fund assets at year-end 2001. Mutual fund retirement assets primarily come from two sources: Individual Retirement Accounts (IRAs) and employer-sponsored defined contribution plans, such as 401(k) plans. Funds hold roughly the same amount of assets in IRAs and employer-sponsored defined contribution plans: $1.17 trillion and $1.19 trillion at year-end 2001, respectively.

Mutual Funds and the IRA Market

IRAs were one of the fastest growing components of the U.S. retirement market between 1990 and 2001, and the mutual fund industry's share of the IRA market has increased from 14 percent in the mid-1980s to 49 percent by year-end 2001.

Assets in IRAs grew during the 1990s primarily due to the investment performance of the securities held in IRA portfolios and rollovers into IRAs from employer-sponsored plans. In addition, legislative changes in the late 1990s introduced new types of IRAs. Furthermore, passage of the Economic Growth and Tax Relief Reconciliation Act (EGTRRA) in 2001 is expected to stimulate savings through IRAs (and other retirement and education savings vehicles). For example, EGTRRA increased the amount investors—especially those aged 50 and older—can contribute to IRAs.

Assets in the IRA Market, 1990–2001[1]
(billions of dollars)

	Bank and Thrift Deposits[2]	Life Insurance Companies[3]	Mutual Funds	Securities Held Directly Through Brokerage Accounts	Total IRA Assets
1990	$266	$40	$140	$190	$637
1991	282	45	188	260	776
1992	275	50	237	311	873
1993	263	61	322	346	993
1994	255	69	350	382	1,056
1995	261	81	476	471	1,288
1996	258	92	597	519	1,467
1997	254	135	776	563	1,728
1998	249	156	974	771	2,150
1999	244	201	1,263	834	2,542
2000	252	202	1,236	817e	2,507e
2001	255	200e	1,168	777e	2,399e

[1]Preliminary data

[2]Bank and thrift deposits include Keogh deposits.

[3]Annuities held by IRAs, excluding variable annuity mutual fund IRA assets.

eEstimated

Note: Components may not add to totals due to rounding.

Sources: Investment Company Institute, Federal Reserve Board, American Council of Life Insurers, and Internal Revenue Service

IRA Investors: Traditional, Roth, and Employer-Sponsored Owners

Approximately four out of 10 U.S. households, or 44.3 million, owned IRAs as of May 2001. IRA households generally are headed by middle-aged individuals with moderate household income who are more likely to hold mutual funds, especially long-term mutual funds, in their IRA portfolios than any other type of investment.

As of May 2001, approximately 34.1 million U.S. households owned "traditional" IRAs—the first type of IRA created (under the Employee Retirement Income Security Act of 1974)—while about 11.9 million U.S. households owned Roth IRAs, first available in 1998. An estimated 8.1 million U.S. households owned employer-sponsored IRAs (SIMPLE IRAs, SEP IRAs, or SAR-SEP IRAs).

Nearly 70 percent of IRA households include mutual funds in their IRAs, with two-thirds investing in long-term mutual funds and 27 percent holding money market mutual funds. Forty percent of IRA households hold individual stocks or bonds in their IRAs, while 29 percent hold annuities and 28 percent, bank deposit accounts.

Traditional IRA households held a median of $30,000 in their traditional IRAs in 2001, typically in two accounts. Forty-four percent of these households had, when surveyed, traditional IRA accounts that included

Types of IRAs and Their Owners

	Year Created	Number of U.S. Households with Type of IRA, 2001	Percent of U.S. Households with Type of IRA, 2001
Traditional IRA	1974 (The Employee Retirement Income Security Act)	34.1 million	32%
Roth IRA	1997 (The Taxpayer Relief Act)	11.9 million	11%
SEP or SAR-SEP IRA	1978 (The Revenue Act)	5.2 million	5%
SIMPLE IRA	1996 (The Small Business Job Protection Act)	4.1 million	4%

Types of Assets Held In IRAs, 2001[1,2]

(percent of U.S. households owning any type of IRA)

Mutual funds	69
Long-term mutual funds[3]	66
Money market mutual funds	27
Individual stocks or bonds	40
Annuities[4]	29
Bank deposit accounts[5]	28
Other	5

[1]Includes traditional IRAs, Roth IRAs, SIMPLE IRAs, SEP-IRAs, and SAR-SEP IRAs.

[2]Multiple responses included.

[3]Includes equity mutual funds, bond mutual funds, and hybrid mutual funds.

[4]Includes variable and fixed annuities.

[5]Includes bank savings accounts, money market deposit accounts, and certificates of deposit.

assets "rolled over" from employer-sponsored retirement plans, and nearly one-third also owned Roth IRAs. Traditional IRA households tended to have greater financial assets but lower income than other types of IRA households. Individuals heading traditional IRA households generally were older and more likely to be retired than individuals heading Roth or employer-sponsored IRA households.

The majority of Roth IRA households owned one Roth IRA account with a median balance of $6,000 in 2001. More than one in three Roth IRA households opened a Roth IRA as their first IRA account. Individuals heading Roth IRA households had a median age of 43 years, and nearly 90 percent were employed.

Households with employer-sponsored IRAs had a median of $48,200 invested in all types of IRAs when surveyed. Sixty-two percent of these households also owned traditional IRAs and 27 percent also owned Roth IRAs. Nearly one-third of individuals heading households with employer-sponsored IRAs were self-employed.

Mutual Fund Assets by Type of Retirement Plan, 1991 and 2001*

1991

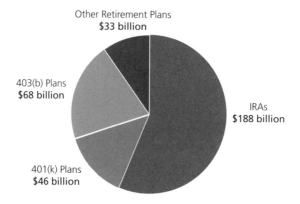

Other Retirement Plans
$33 billion

403(b) Plans
$68 billion

IRAs
$188 billion

401(k) Plans
$46 billion

Total: $335 billion

2001*

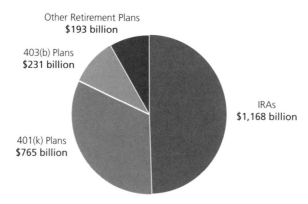

Other Retirement Plans
$193 billion

403(b) Plans
$231 billion

IRAs
$1,168 billion

401(k) Plans
$765 billion

Total: $2,356 billion

*Preliminary data

Note: Components may not add to totals due to rounding.

Sources: Investment Company Institute, Federal Reserve Board, Internal Revenue Service, and Department of Labor

Assets in 401(k) Plans, 1990–2001*

(billions of dollars)

	Mutual Fund 401(k) Plan Assets	Other 401(k) Plan Assets	Total
1990	$35	$350	$385
1991	46	394	440
1992	82	471	553
1993	140	476	616
1994	184	491	675
1995	266	598	864
1996	349	712	1,061
1997	473	791	1,264
1998	605	936	1,541
1999	793	1,018[e]	1,811[e]
2000	783	1,025[e]	1,809[e]
2001	765	990[e]	1,754[e]

*Preliminary data

[e]Estimated

Note: Components may not add to totals due to rounding.

Sources: Investment Company Institute, Federal Reserve Board, and Department of Labor

Mutual Funds and the Employer-Sponsored Pension Market

The mutual fund industry's share of the employer-sponsored pension plan market increased from 2 percent in 1990 to 14 percent at year-end 2001. At the end of 2001, mutual funds accounted for $1.2 trillion of the estimated $8.5 trillion employer-sponsored pension market.

As with the IRA market, Congress's passage of the Economic Growth and Tax Relief Reconciliation Act (EGTRRA) in 2001 increases the amount investors—particularly those age 50 and older—can contribute to employer-sponsored plans, and is expected to help individuals save more for retirement.

Mutual fund assets held in employer-sponsored retirement accounts totaled $1.2 trillion in 2001, a decrease of $51 billion, or 4 percent, from 2000. Mutual funds accounted for approximately 14 percent of the overall employer-sponsored pension market at year-end 2001. The employer-sponsored pension market is comprised of $1.9 trillion in assets in private defined benefit pension funds, $2.5 trillion in private defined contribution

Average Asset Allocation for All 401(k) Plan Balances, 2000
(percent)

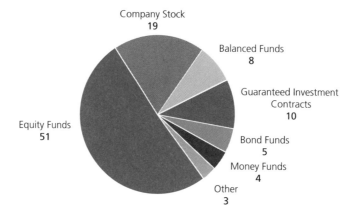

Company Stock
19

Balanced Funds
8

Guaranteed Investment
Contracts
10

Equity Funds
51

Bond Funds
5

Money Funds
4

Other
3

Note: Funds include mutual funds and other pooled investments.

Source: Tabulations from EBRI/ICI Participant-Directed Retirement Plan Data Collection Project

pension funds (and 457 plans), $2.2 trillion in state and local government employee retirement funds, $1.2 trillion in annuity reserves, and $0.8 trillion in federal government defined benefit plans.

Mutual Funds and the Defined Contribution Market

The most important source of mutual fund assets in the employer-sponsored pension plan market is defined contribution plans, especially 401(k) plans. At year-end 2001, 67 percent, or $765 billion, of mutual fund defined contribution plan assets were held in 401(k) plans. Mutual funds' share of the 401(k) market increased from 9 percent in 1990 to an estimated 44 percent at year-end 2001. Mutual fund assets in 403(b) plans were about 20 percent of mutual fund assets in defined contribution plans at year-end 2001, or $231 billion. The remaining mutual fund assets in defined contribution plans were in 457 plans, Keoghs, and other defined contribution plans without 401(k) features.

401(k) Participants: Asset Allocations, Balances, and Loans

For many American workers, 401(k) plan accounts have become an important part of their retirement planning. The income these accounts are expected to provide in retirement depends, in part, on the asset allocation decisions of plan participants.

According to research conducted by ICI and the Employee Benefit Research Institute (EBRI), asset allocation behavior among 401(k) plan participants can vary widely, depending on a variety of factors. For example, younger participants tend to allocate a larger portion of their account balances to equity funds (which include equity mutual funds and other pooled equity investments), while older participants are more likely to invest in guaranteed investment contracts (GICs) and bond funds. On average, individuals in their twenties invested 61.4 percent of their assets in equity funds, 8.6 percent in balanced funds, 4.0 percent in GICs, 4.3 percent in bond funds, 4.3 percent in money funds, and 15.4 percent in company stock. By comparison, individuals in their sixties invested 39.8 percent of their assets in equity funds, 8.0 percent in balanced funds, 19.3 percent in GICs, 7.7 percent in bond funds, 5.4 percent in money funds, and 16.3 percent in company stock.

Average 401(k) Account Balance by Age and Tenure, 2000

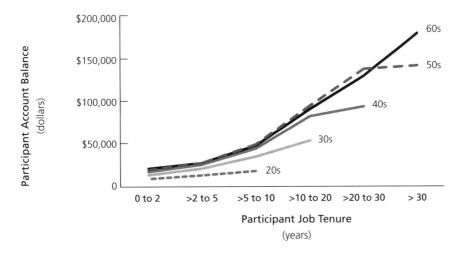

Note: See page 109 for data points on this chart.

Source: Tabulations from EBRI/ICI Participant-Directed Retirement Plan Data Collection Project

The average 401(k) account balance, excluding plan loans, was $49,024 at year-end 2000. Workers in their sixties with at least 30 years of job tenure at their current employer had an average 401(k) account balance of $177,289.

Most 401(k) participants do not borrow from their plans. At year-end 2000, only 18 percent of those eligible for loans had loans outstanding. The average unpaid loan balance for these participants represented about 14 percent of their account balances (net of the unpaid loan balances).

Types of Funds Used by Retirement Plan Investors

Of the $2.4 trillion in mutual fund retirement assets at year-end 2001, $1.7 trillion, or 71 percent, were invested in U.S. domestic or foreign equity funds. U.S. domestic equity funds alone constitute $1.5 trillion, or 63 percent, of mutual fund retirement assets. By comparison, only about 49 percent of overall fund industry assets—including retirement and nonretirement accounts—are invested in domestic and foreign equity funds.

Approximately $482 billion, or 20 percent, of mutual fund retirement assets are invested in fixed-income funds: bond or money market funds. Bond funds hold $220 billion, or 9 percent, of mutual fund retirement assets, and money market funds account for $262 billion, or 11 percent.

Mutual Fund Retirement Assets by Type of Fund, 2001[1]
(billions of dollars)

	Equity		Bond	Hybrid	Money Market	Total
	Domestic	Foreign				
IRAs	$696	$98	$116	$95	$163	$1,168
401(k) Plans	508	60	53	80	63	765
403(b) Plans	181	14	10	12	15	231
Other Employer-Sponsored Plans[2]	105	14	41	13	21	193
Total	$1,489	$185	$220	$200	$262	$2,356

[1]*Preliminary data*

[2]*Includes 457 plans, private defined benefit plans, state and local government employee retirement funds, Keoghs, and other defined contribution plans without 401(k) features.*

Note: Components may not add to totals due to rounding.

The remaining $200 billion, or approximately 8 percent, of mutual fund retirement assets are held in hybrid funds, which invest in a mix of equity and fixed-income securities and derivative instruments.

Education Saving: Section 529 Plans and Coverdell Education Savings Accounts

The enactment of EGTRRA in 2001 is expected to stimulate new investments in education savings vehicles. Historically, the demand for these products has been modest since their introduction in the 1990s, partly attributable to investors' lack of familiarity with them and because of their

Section 529 Savings Plan Assets, 1998–2001
(billions of dollars)

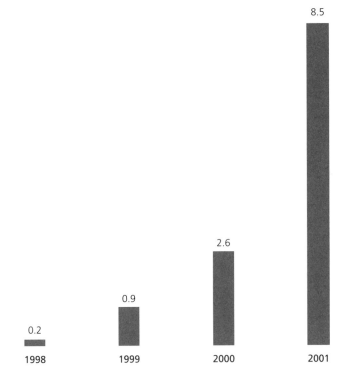

Note: Data were estimated for a few individual state observations in order to construct a continuous time series.

Sources: Investment Company Institute, College Savings Plans Network, SavingforCollege.com, individual states, and investment managers

limited availability. In addition, some provisions of these plans served to limit their appeal as education savings vehicles.

The new law greatly enhances the attractiveness of both Section 529 plans and Coverdell Education Savings Accounts by allowing greater contributions and flexibility in the plans. The maximum annual investment levels for Coverdell accounts increase in 2002 to $2,000 from $500 in 2001, and tax-free withdrawals from these accounts are allowed for qualified higher-education, elementary, and secondary schooling expenses. The new law also allows tax-free distributions from Section 529 savings plans for qualified higher-education expenses. Previously, withdrawals from these accounts were generally taxed at the rate of the beneficiary—usually a child or grandchild. In another change, contributors now will be able to move their 529 plan investments from one state's plan to another once a year without having to change beneficiaries.

Assets in Section 529 savings plans more than tripled in 2001, increasing from $2.6 billion at year-end 2000 to $8.5 billion by year-end 2001. The number of accounts rose to more than one million, and the average account size was approximately $6,300.

About ICI Data

ICI is a source for information on investment company statistical trends.
Institute staff collect, compile, verify for accuracy, and release to government agencies, the media, the public, and ICI members a wide range of
statistics on approximately 8,300 mutual funds, 450 closed-end funds, 10
unit investment trust sponsors, and 100 exchange-traded funds in the U.S.
investment company industry. The Institute also collects data on foreign
investment companies from industry associations around the world.

The impetus for ICI's data collection efforts began in the summer of
1940—following the enactment of the Investment Company Act—when
investment company leaders first formed a committee to monitor industry
progress and trends. In 1944, that committee began collecting fund
statistics. Mutual fund assets have grown from $1 billion in 1945 to nearly
$7 trillion as of December 31, 2001.

On the following pages, you will find historical data on investment
companies. The first five sections of data represent aggregate statistics
reported to ICI from individual U.S. mutual funds representing
95 percent of the U.S. industry's assets. The sixth section provides data
on open-end investment companies from around the world, and the
seventh section features data on other types of U.S. investment companies:
closed-end funds, unit investment trusts, and exchange-traded funds.

U.S. Mutual Fund Data

The U.S. mutual fund data section begins with a breakdown of U.S.
industry totals in Section One, including information on fund assets,
accounts, and the number of funds. U.S. industry totals are broken down
from short- and long-term categories into five separate ones: equity funds,
hybrid funds, bond funds, taxable money market funds, and tax-exempt
money market funds.

In Sections Two and Three, U.S. mutual fund data are classified according to two broad categories: long-term funds and short-term, or money market, funds. Long-term fund data are classified according to three broad fund categories—equity, bond, and hybrid—and further categorized into 29 more specific investment objective groupings. Money market funds are categorized into four taxable and tax-exempt investment objective groupings.

U.S. industry data do not provide total sales figures that combine long-term and short-term fund sales. Because of the special nature of short-term funds and the huge, continuous inflows and outflows of money they experience, it would be misleading to add their sales figures to those of long-term funds.

Section Four examines exchanges for all funds in the U.S. industry; Section Five looks at institutional investors in the U.S. industry.

DATA SECTION

Table of Contents

Total Industry Net Assets, Number of Funds, and Shareholder Accounts

Year	Total Net Assets (millions)	Number of Funds	Number of Shareholder Accounts
1940	$448.0	68	296,056
1945	1,284.2	73	497,875
1950	2,530.6	98	938,651
1955	7,837.5	125	2,085,325
1960	17,025.7	161	4,897,600
1965	35,220.2	170	6,709,343
1970	47,618.1	361	10,690,312
1971	55,045.3	392	10,900,952
1972	59,830.6	410	10,635,287
1973	46,518.5	421	10,330,862
1974	35,776.8	431	10,074,191
1975	45,874.4	426	9,876,082
1976	51,276.6	452	9,060,089
1977	48,936.9	477	8,692,601
1978	55,837.7	505	8,658,324
1979	94,511.3	524	9,790,018
1980	134,760.9	564	12,087,646
1981	241,365.4	665	17,498,938
1982	296,678.1	857	21,448,409
1983	292,985.1	1,026	24,604,659
1984	370,680.0	1,243	27,635,660
1985	495,385.1	1,528	34,098,401
1986	715,667.8	1,835	45,373,627
1987	769,171.9	2,312	53,717,241
1988	809,370.5	2,737	54,056,016
1989	980,671.1	2,935	57,559,770
1990	1,065,190.2	3,079	61,947,955
1991	1,393,185.3	3,403	68,334,053
1992	1,642,536.7	3,824	79,932,211
1993	2,069,963.2	4,534	93,213,735
1994	2,155,324.9	5,325	114,383,364
1995	2,811,292.2	5,725	131,219,225
1996	3,525,800.8	6,248	150,045,888
1997	4,468,200.6	6,684	170,367,063
1998	5,525,209.3	7,314	194,147,377
1999	6,846,339.2	7,791	227,260,442
2000	6,964,667.0	8,155	244,409,464
2001	6,974,975.9	8,307	247,841,168

Note: The data contain a series break beginning in 1984. At that time, data for funds that invest in other mutual funds were excluded from the series.

Total Industry Net Assets
(billions of dollars)

Year	Equity Funds	Bond & Income Funds	Taxable Money Market Funds	Tax-Exempt Money Market Funds	Total
1960	$16.0	$1.0	–	–	$17.0
1965	32.8	2.5	–	–	35.2
1970	45.1	2.5	–	–	47.6
1971	51.6	3.4	–	–	55.0
1972	55.9	3.9	–	–	59.8
1973	43.0	3.5	–	–	46.5
1974	30.9	3.2	$1.7	–	35.8
1975	37.5	4.7	3.7	–	45.9
1976	39.2	8.4	3.7	–	51.3
1977	34.0	11.0	3.9	–	48.9
1978	32.7	12.3	10.9	–	55.9
1979	35.9	13.1	45.2	$0.3	94.5
1980	44.4	14.0	74.5	1.9	134.8
1981	41.2	14.0	181.9	4.3	241.4
1982	53.7	23.2	206.6	13.2	296.7
1983	77.0	36.6	162.5	16.8	292.9

	Equity Funds	Hybrid Funds	Bond Funds	Taxable Money Market Funds	Tax-Exempt Money Market Funds	Total
1984	$79.7	$11.2	$46.2	$209.7	$23.8	$370.7
1985	111.3	17.6	122.6	207.5	36.3	495.4
1986	154.4	25.8	243.3	228.3	63.8	715.7
1987	175.5	29.3	248.4	254.7	61.4	769.2
1988	189.4	26.3	255.7	272.3	65.7	809.4
1989	245.0	35.6	271.9	358.7	69.4	980.7
1990	239.5	36.1	291.3	414.7	83.6	1,065.2
1991	404.7	52.2	393.8	452.6	89.9	1,393.2
1992	514.1	78.0	504.2	451.4	94.8	1,642.5
1993	740.7	144.5	619.5	461.9	103.4	2,070.0
1994	852.8	164.4	527.2	500.6	110.4	2,155.3
1995	1,249.1	210.3	598.9	630.0	123.0	2,811.3
1996	1,726.0	252.6	645.4	762.0	139.8	3,525.8
1997	2,368.0	317.1	724.2	898.1	160.8	4,468.2
1998	2,978.2	364.7	830.6	1,163.2	188.5	5,525.2
1999	4,041.9	378.8	812.5	1,408.7	204.4	6,846.3
2000	3,962.0	346.3	811.1	1,607.2	238.1	6,964.7
2001	3,418.2	346.3	925.1	2,012.9	272.4	6,974.9

Note: The data contain a series break beginning in 1984. All funds were reclassified in 1984 and a separate category was created for hybrid funds. At the same time, data for funds that invest in other mutual funds were excluded from the series.

Components may not sum to the total due to rounding.

Total Industry Shareholder Accounts
(millions)

Year	Equity Funds	Bond & Income Funds	Taxable Money Market Funds	Tax-Exempt Money Market Funds	Total
1978	6.8	1.4	0.5	–	8.7
1979	6.1	1.4	2.3	–	9.8
1980	5.8	1.5	4.8	–	12.1
1981	5.7	1.5	10.3	–	17.5
1982	6.2	2.0	13.1	0.1	21.4
1983	9.2	2.8	12.3	0.3	24.6

	Equity Funds	Hybrid Funds	Bond Funds	Taxable Money Market Funds	Tax-Exempt Money Market Funds	Total
1984	9.6	1.0	3.2	13.6	0.3	27.6
1985	11.1	1.3	6.8	14.4	0.5	34.1
1986	15.5	2.1	11.5	15.7	0.7	45.4
1987	20.4	2.7	12.9	16.8	0.8	53.7
1988	19.7	2.6	13.3	17.6	0.9	54.1
1989	20.3	2.7	13.2	20.2	1.1	57.6
1990	22.2	3.2	13.6	21.6	1.4	61.9
1991	25.6	3.6	15.5	21.9	1.7	68.3
1992	32.7	4.5	19.0	21.8	1.9	79.9
1993	42.3	6.9	20.5	21.6	2.0	93.2
1994	57.9	10.3	20.8	23.3	2.0	114.4
1995	69.3	10.9	20.8	27.9	2.3	131.2
1996	85.4	12.0	20.4	29.9	2.3	150.0
1997	101.8	12.9	20.1	33.0	2.7	170.4
1998	119.9	13.8	21.6	36.4	2.4	194.1
1999	148.3	14.2	21.1	41.2	2.4	227.3
2000	163.7	13.1	19.5	45.5	2.7	244.4
2001	164.8	14.2	21.6	44.4	2.8	247.8

Note: The data contain a series break beginning in 1984. All funds were reclassified in 1984 and a separate category was created for hybrid funds. At the same time, data for funds that invest in other mutual funds were excluded from the series.

Components may not sum to the total due to rounding.

Total Number of Funds

Year	Equity Funds	Bond & Income Funds	Taxable Money Market Funds	Tax-Exempt Money Market Funds	Total
1970	323	38	–	–	361
1971	350	42	–	–	392
1972	364	46	–	–	410
1973	366	55	–	–	421
1974	343	73	15	–	431
1975	314	76	36	–	426
1976	302	102	48	–	452
1977	296	131	50	–	477
1978	294	150	61	–	505
1979	289	159	76	–	524
1980	288	170	96	10	564
1981	306	180	159	20	665
1982	340	199	281	37	857
1983	396	257	307	66	1,026

	Equity Funds	Hybrid Funds	Bond Funds	Taxable Money Market Funds	Tax-Exempt Money Market Funds	Total
1984	459	89	270	329	96	1,243
1985	562	103	403	348	112	1,528
1986	678	121	549	360	127	1,835
1987	824	164	781	389	154	2,312
1988	1,006	179	942	434	176	2,737
1989	1,069	189	1,004	470	203	2,935
1990	1,099	193	1,046	506	235	3,079
1991	1,191	212	1,180	553	267	3,403
1992	1,325	235	1,400	585	279	3,824
1993	1,586	282	1,746	628	292	4,534
1994	1,886	361	2,115	646	317	5,325
1995	2,139	412	2,177	674	323	5,725
1996	2,570	466	2,224	666	322	6,248
1997	2,951	501	2,219	682	331	6,684
1998	3,513	525	2,250	685	341	7,314
1999	3,952	532	2,262	702	343	7,791
2000	4,385	523	2,208	703	336	8,155
2001	4,717	484	2,091	689	326	8,307

Note: The data contain a series break beginning in 1984. All funds were reclassified in 1984 and a separate category was created for hybrid funds. At the same time, data for funds that invest in other mutual funds were excluded from the series.

An Overview:
Shareholder Accounts, Total Net Assets, and Liquid Assets
of Equity, Hybrid, and Bond Funds

Year	Number of Reporting Funds	Number of Accounts (thousands)	Net Assets (billions of dollars)	Liquid Assets (billions of dollars)
1970	361	10,690.3	$47.6	$3.1
1971	392	10,901.0	55.0	2.6
1972	410	10,635.3	59.8	2.6
1973	421	10,330.9	46.5	3.4
1974	416	9,970.4	34.1	3.4
1975	390	9,667.3	42.2	3.2
1976	404	8,879.4	47.6	2.4
1977	427	8,515.1	45.0	3.3
1978	444	8,190.6	45.0	4.5
1979	446	7,482.2	49.0	4.7
1980	458	7,325.5	58.4	5.3
1981	486	7,175.5	55.2	5.3
1982	539	8,190.3	76.9	6.0
1983	653	12,065.0	113.6	8.3
1984	818	13,791.0	137.1	12.2
1985	1,068	19,163.8	251.6	20.6
1986	1,348	29,060.5	423.5	30.6
1987	1,769	36,042.5	453.1	37.9
1988	2,127	35,486.2	471.4	45.0
1989	2,262	36,245.5	552.6	44.6
1990	2,338	38,979.1	566.8	48.4
1991	2,583	44,778.1	850.7	60.4
1992	2,960	56,285.0	1,096.3	74.0
1993	3,614	69,628.4	1,504.6	99.4
1994	4,362	89,004.7	1,544.3	120.4
1995	4,728	101,082.4	2,058.3	141.8
1996	5,260	117,846.0	2,624.0	152.0
1997	5,671	134,743.0	3,409.3	198.8
1998	6,288	155,300.0	4,173.5	191.4
1999	6,746	183,644.9	5,233.2	219.1
2000	7,116	196,271.0	5,119.4	277.2
2001	7,292	200,604.7	4,689.6	219.5

Note: Figures for shareholder accounts represent combined totals for member companies; duplications have not been eliminated. The data contain a series break beginning in 1984. All funds were reclassified in 1984 and a separate category was created for hybrid funds. At the same time, data for funds that invest in other mutual funds were excluded from the series.

Total Net Assets of Equity, Hybrid, and Bond Funds
by Investment Objective
(millions of dollars)

	1999	2000	2001
Total Net Assets	$5,233,193.6	$5,119,386.2	$4,689,628.0
Aggressive Growth	$623,855.6	$667,718.9	$576,241.9
Growth	1,286,616.7	1,250,869.1	1,047,517.4
Sector	204,588.1	235,127.7	173,602.2
World Equity–Emerging Markets	22,101.0	15,406.8	13,677.3
World Equity–Global	236,389.6	228,025.0	182,983.8
World Equity–International	276,226.8	262,065.9	206,295.0
World Equity–Regional	50,537.2	37,171.2	25,840.2
Growth and Income	1,202,141.2	1,137,217.4	1,066,633.4
Income Equity	139,433.8	128,320.0	125,382.1
Total Equity Funds	**$4,041,890.0**	**$3,961,922.0**	**$3,418,173.3**
Asset Allocation	$39,338.1	$36,808.1	$34,338.3
Balanced	184,294.0	172,675.5	179,659.3
Flexible Portfolio	94,517.1	89,007.9	80,946.2
Income–Mixed	60,660.3	47,784.3	51,386.8
Total Hybrid Funds	**$378,809.5**	**$346,275.8**	**$346,330.6**
Corporate Bond–General	$31,280.6	$29,189.2	$33,023.5
Corporate Bond–Intermediate-term	73,552.2	61,098.3	70,401.3
Corporate Bond–Short-Term	52,848.6	50,348.2	57,543.5
High-Yield Bond	116,904.5	90,282.7	94,275.7
World Bond–Global General	14,919.1	12,692.5	12,400.4
World Bond–Global Short-Term	4,044.3	3,257.9	2,672.6
World Bond–Other	3,980.5	3,990.0	3,993.3
Government Bond–General	34,653.5	35,004.0	40,706.0
Government Bond–Intermediate-Term	24,561.8	24,587.5	29,299.3
Government Bond–Short-Term	19,385.3	16,923.5	20,870.1
Government Bond–Mortgage-Backed	59,981.2	56,820.4	73,367.6
Strategic Income	104,902.6	149,149.3	191,552.9
State Municipal Bond–General	117,829.2	123,337.4	130,913.4
State Municipal Bond–Short-Term	10,059.7	9,382.9	10,077.1
National Municipal Bond–General	112,294.7	120,435.4	124,864.1
National Municipal Bond–Short-Term	31,296.3	24,689.2	29,163.3
Total Bond Funds	**$812,494.1**	**$811,188.4**	**$925,124.1**

Note: Data for funds that invest in other mutual funds were excluded from the series.

Liquid Assets of Equity, Hybrid, and Bond Funds by Investment Objective

(millions of dollars)

	1999	2000	2001
Total Liquid Assets	**$219,097.9**	**$277,158.5**	**$219,514.2**
Aggressive Growth	$23,491.9	$44,156.4	$28,070.3
Growth	60,079.1	69,600.4	54,896.0
Sector	11,581.8	15,917.7	10,035.7
World Equity–Emerging Markets	651.1	947.2	578.2
World Equity–Global	14,790.8	21,731.1	13,049.7
World Equity–International	13,846.5	17,514.8	12,687.9
World Equity–Regional	1,754.4	1,372.1	743.2
Growth and Income	41,778.4	49,884.5	46,347.7
Income Equity	6,717.9	6,836.3	4,283.6
Total Equity Funds	**$174,691.9**	**$227,960.5**	**$170,692.3**
Asset Allocation	$3,029.2	$2,315.0	$2,409.6
Balanced	7,667.3	8,192.6	10,039.6
Flexible Portfolio	7,525.4	9,258.6	7,237.7
Income–Mixed	2,434.2	4,002.5	4,642.8
Total Hybrid Funds	**$20,656.1**	**$23,768.7**	**$24,329.7**
Corporate Bond–General	$677.8	$539.6	$641.4
Corporate Bond–Intermediate-Term	2,051.6	1,299.7	2,552.9
Corporate Bond–Short-Term	5,877.9	4,754.0	5,947.0
High-Yield Bond	5,035.2	7,606.9	6,477.2
World Bond–Global General	1,022.2	497.3	392.4
World Bond–Global Short-Term	312.6	276.6	130.5
World Bond–Other	258.5	83.0	112.7
Government Bond–General	(633.4)	383.1	693.2
Government Bond–Intermediate-Term	472.6	1,076.3	1,114.0
Government Bond–Short-Term	(763.0)	101.5	1,357.5
Government Bond–Mortgage-Backed	(5,432.5)	(5,087.9)	(3,711.5)
Strategic Income	8,589.7	4,671.5	758.2
State Municipal Bond–General	2,402.4	3,703.5	2,661.7
State Municipal Bond–Short-Term	316.0	432.8	535.3
National Municipal Bond–General	2,326.6	3,309.4	2,893.6
National Municipal Bond–Short-Term	1,235.7	1,782.0	1,936.1
Total Bond Funds	**$23,749.9**	**$25,429.3**	**$24,492.2**

Note: Data for funds that invest in other mutual funds were excluded from the series.

Section Two: U.S. Industry Long-Term Funds

Liquid Asset Ratio—Equity Funds

Year	January	February	March	April	May	June	July	August	September	October	November	December
1975	8.8	9.7	8.2	7.8	7.5	6.8	7.1	7.5	7.8	7.4	7.6	7.6
1976	6.0	5.5	5.1	4.8	5.2	4.8	4.6	4.7	4.5	4.5	5.0	4.9
1977	5.3	6.0	6.5	6.1	6.6	6.2	6.8	7.5	7.9	8.2	8.0	7.5
1978	8.5	10.2	10.3	10.1	9.5	9.2	8.0	6.9	6.5	6.7	7.9	8.2
1979	8.1	8.9	8.3	8.5	8.8	8.7	8.7	8.5	8.2	7.9	8.2	7.9
1980	8.5	9.0	9.2	9.5	10.4	10.1	10.4	10.3	9.8	9.7	9.3	9.1
1981	8.1	8.4	8.3	8.5	9.0	9.0	8.7	9.4	10.4	10.8	11.4	10.5
1982	10.5	10.4	10.8	10.5	11.4	12.2	11.0	10.1	9.2	8.9	8.4	8.6
1983	9.7	9.5	9.9	9.9	9.5	9.4	9.0	7.7	8.6	7.9	8.7	7.8
1984	7.9	8.5	9.2	9.5	9.4	9.8	10.2	9.7	9.3	8.8	9.2	9.1
1985	8.7	9.1	8.4	9.2	8.9	8.9	9.4	10.0	10.1	10.9	10.0	9.4
1986	9.8	8.9	9.3	10.1	9.7	9.3	9.9	9.7	10.3	9.9	9.6	9.5
1987	9.7	9.5	9.0	10.2	9.4	9.3	9.3	8.8	9.2	10.5	11.3	9.3
1988	10.3	10.0	10.4	10.9	10.6	10.3	10.6	10.6	10.7	9.9	9.6	9.4
1989	9.3	8.9	8.6	8.8	9.3	9.9	10.0	10.3	10.2	10.7	11.1	10.4
1990	11.5	11.6	11.9	12.5	11.3	10.7	10.7	11.9	12.8	12.9	12.4	11.4
1991	9.7	9.5	8.7	8.4	8.5	8.0	7.7	7.2	7.4	7.8	8.4	7.6
1992	7.1	7.2	7.8	8.3	8.1	8.7	8.8	9.1	8.5	8.6	8.8	8.3
1993	8.2	8.8	9.1	9.5	8.5	8.4	8.5	8.0	7.8	8.1	8.0	7.8
1994	8.2	8.6	7.8	8.0	8.4	8.3	8.6	8.3	8.2	8.3	8.9	8.3
1995	8.4	8.2	7.5	7.4	7.4	7.1	7.1	7.2	7.0	7.5	7.9	7.8
1996	8.1	7.4	7.0	7.0	6.6	6.5	7.0	7.1	6.7	6.4	6.3	6.2
1997	6.6	6.5	6.9	7.1	6.9	6.4	5.9	6.1	6.0	6.2	6.5	6.1
1998	6.4	5.7	5.2	4.8	4.9	5.2	5.2	6.0	6.3	5.9	5.5	4.8
1999	4.9	4.9	4.6	4.8	4.9	4.8	4.8	4.8	4.9	5.0	4.6	4.3
2000	4.4	4.4	4.0	4.9	5.2	4.8	5.0	4.7	5.3	5.9	6.5	5.8
2001	5.6	5.9	5.8	5.5	5.4	5.6	5.6	5.5	5.6	5.6	5.6	5.0

Note: The data contain a series break beginning in 1984. At that time, data for funds that invest in other mutual funds were excluded from the series.

Distribution of Mutual Fund Assets in Equity, Hybrid, and Bond Funds

(millions of dollars)

Year	Total Net Assets	Net Cash & Equivalent	Corporate Bonds	Preferred Stocks	Common Stocks	Municipal Bonds	Long-Term U.S. Gov't	Other
1980	$58,400	$5,321	$6,582	$531	$41,561	$2,866	$1,433	$106
1981	55,207	5,277	7,489	399	36,649	3,046	2,147	200
1982	76,841	6,040	10,833	1,628	47,720	6,797	3,752	71
1983	113,599	8,343	13,052	1,474	72,942	13,368	3,894	526
1984	137,126	12,181	14,929	1,655	81,485	16,882	9,661	333
1985	251,583	20,593	24,987	3,777	109,774	38,174	53,449	829
1986	423,516	30,611	47,246	7,377	153,449	70,778	111,384	2,671
1987	453,076	37,930	41,592	5,557	176,079	68,464	119,655	3,799
1988	471,417	44,980	54,364	5,670	173,440	86,016	103,605	3,342
1989	552,578	44,603	52,830	4,572	240,780	84,831	117,850	7,112
1990	566,849	48,440	45,365	3,339	213,112	117,084	128,153	11,356
1991	850,744	60,385	86,930	6,606	375,005	149,533	163,284	9,001
1992	1,096,342	73,984	115,441	10,521	474,765	191,779	225,280	4,572
1993	1,504,644	99,436	165,589	16,209	696,045	249,163	272,248	5,954
1994	1,544,320	120,430	155,158	16,463	807,250	211,127	223,070	10,822
1995	2,058,275	141,755	190,880	16,828	1,198,381	245,331	259,076	6,024
1996	2,623,994	151,988	237,988	21,165	1,696,935	245,182	265,110	5,626
1997	3,409,315	198,826	292,903	29,470	2,328,873	266,327	282,061	10,855
1998	4,173,531	191,393	389,056	25,709	2,978,590	292,505	286,505	9,773
1999	5,233,194	219,098	387,669	30,911	4,028,607	267,438	294,270	5,201
2000	5,119,386	277,159	349,096	27,111	3,883,256	269,179	309,631	3,954
2001	4,689,628	219,514	376,368	22,280	3,404,186	289,689	375,902	1,689

Note: The data contain a series break beginning in 1984. All funds were reclassified in 1984 and a separate category was created for hybrid funds. At the same time, data for funds that invest in other mutual funds were excluded from the series.

Net New Cash Flow* by Investment Objective
(millions of dollars)

	1999	2000	2001
Total Net New Cash Flow	$169,779.9	$228,874.0	$129,152.1
Aggressive Growth	$34,340.2	$129,318.5	$19,015.3
Growth	97,001.6	119,078.4	6,081.2
Sector	28,948.3	62,310.5	(7,917.0)
World Equity–Emerging Markets	763.9	108.5	(1,249.9)
World Equity–Global	3,091.2	22,688.8	(10,342.0)
World Equity–International	5,986.8	31,461.5	(6,056.6)
World Equity–Regional	1,382.5	(4,465.4)	(4,153.5)
Growth and Income	30,660.6	(32,079.8)	31,986.0
Income Equity	(14,509.4)	(19,056.3)	4,564.7
Total Equity Funds	$187,665.7	$309,364.7	$31,928.2
Asset Allocation	($5,438.5)	($3,158.1)	($424.7)
Balanced	(140.2)	(12,271.7)	9,711.5
Flexible Portfolio	(2,387.3)	(7,181.9)	(2,357.2)
Income–Mixed	(5,839.3)	(8,116.0)	2,590.5
Total Hybrid Funds	($13,805.3)	($30,727.7)	$9,520.1
Corporate Bond–General	($383.1)	($1,750.2)	$2,284.4
Corporate Bond–Intermediate-Term	3,722.9	(2,514.3)	5,484.0
Corporate Bond–Short-Term	2,855.1	(3,472.0)	3,380.1
High-Yield Bond	(2,545.8)	(12,305.9)	7,195.5
World Bond–Global General	(1,423.1)	(869.8)	(429.0)
World Bond–Global Short-Term	(559.1)	(609.3)	(313.6)
World Bond–Other	(196.3)	(728.4)	(279.8)
Government Bond–General	(2,620.0)	(3,283.4)	5,341.9
Government Bond–Intermediate-Term	846.2	(2,297.8)	3,451.2
Government Bond–Short-Term	(619.1)	(3,440.6)	3,610.1
Government Bond–Mortgage-Backed	191.5	(7,321.9)	15,468.6
Strategic Income	8,801.5	2,968.0	30,918.5
State Municipal Bond–General	(4,602.4)	(5,740.5)	5,675.8
State Municipal Bond–Short-Term	19.5	227.8	954.8
National Municipal Bond–General	(7,004.1)	(8,545.4)	2,116.9
National Municipal Bond–Short-Term	(564.2)	(79.3)	2,844.4
Total Bond Funds	($4,080.5)	($49,763.0)	$87,703.8

*Net new cash flow is the dollar value of new sales minus redemptions, combined with net exchanges.

Note: Data for funds that invest in other mutual funds were excluded from the series.

Net New Cash Flow* and Total Net Assets of Equity Funds
(millions of dollars)

	Net New Cash Flow	Total Net Assets
1999		
January	$17,221.8	$3,073,611.9
February	767.1	2,976,057.7
March	12,570.4	3,109,136.5
April	25,849.5	3,265,041.1
May	14,953.8	3,220,462.4
June	18,870.3	3,424,674.2
July	12,335.1	3,367,283.3
August	9,475.2	3,342,455.2
September	11,246.5	3,301,188.3
October	20,964.6	3,506,880.2
November	18,526.8	3,672,348.4
December	24,884.6	4,041,890.1
Total	**$187,665.7**	**$4,041,890.1**
2000		
January	$44,541.0	$3,956,475.2
February	55,609.6	4,231,187.1
March	40,220.3	4,441,463.1
April	35,505.0	4,246,875.6
May	17,224.2	4,106,403.4
June	21,962.8	4,320,124.0
July	16,760.3	4,246,154.9
August	24,064.6	4,571,681.5
September	17,618.2	4,388,624.3
October	19,286.3	4,283,751.2
November	5,032.8	3,854,652.1
December	11,539.6	3,961,921.9
Total	**$309,364.7**	**$3,961,921.9**
2001		
January	$24,936.9	$4,093,533.7
February	(3,285.0)	3,688,854.0
March	(20,694.3)	3,402,940.5
April	19,103.1	3,715,684.3
May	18,383.2	3,744,556.2
June	10,850.6	3,677,236.7
July	(1,278.3)	3,589,269.6
August	(4,953.3)	3,382,577.2
September	(29,962.0)	3,019,008.8
October	873.1	3,111,176.0
November	15,152.2	3,348,579.5
December	2,802.0	3,418,173.5
Total	**$31,928.2**	**$3,418,173.5**

*Net new cash flow is the dollar value of new sales minus redemptions, combined with net exchanges.

Note: Data for funds that invest in other mutual funds were excluded from the series.

Net New Cash Flow* and Total Net Assets of Hybrid Funds
(millions of dollars)

	Net New Cash Flow	Total Net Assets
1999		
January	$413.5	$365,886.8
February	(1,250.5)	357,311.9
March	(1,141.7)	363,443.9
April	(530.6)	377,171.0
May	(414.4)	370,888.0
June	(415.5)	380,644.0
July	(425.2)	373,581.3
August	(1,113.0)	368,672.4
September	(1,030.2)	362,420.8
October	(958.8)	370,558.7
November	(2,732.1)	372,151.5
December	(4,206.8)	378,809.5
Total	**($13,805.3)**	**$378,809.5**
2000		
January	($6,268.4)	$350,899.1
February	(5,260.6)	341,864.8
March	(5,345.7)	353,458.8
April	(2,054.2)	346,124.3
May	(2,186.0)	343,583.7
June	(1,911.4)	347,254.6
July	(1,722.5)	348,579.6
August	(1,746.7)	358,560.2
September	(1,740.4)	350,851.0
October	(1,220.9)	349,858.2
November	(304.5)	338,781.7
December	(966.4)	346,275.8
Total	**($30,727.7)**	**$346,275.8**
2001		
January	$2,509.8	$354,882.2
February	1,263.4	344,901.9
March	(403.2)	333,735.3
April	1,229.9	348,036.7
May	867.9	352,649.2
June	1,228.8	349,873.5
July	1,287.8	351,676.5
August	(732.4)	342,565.6
September	(1,274.0)	324,083.3
October	1,550.2	330,329.1
November	955.6	342,952.3
December	1,036.3	346,330.5
Total	**$9,520.1**	**$346,330.5**

*Net new cash flow is the dollar value of new sales minus redemptions, combined with net exchanges.

Note: Data for funds that invest in other mutual funds were excluded from the series.

Net New Cash Flow* and Total Net Assets of Bond Funds
(millions of dollars)

	Net New Cash Flow	Total Net Assets
1999		
January	$8,513.9	$846,924.9
February	4,608.8	845,050.4
March	6,321.8	855,340.9
April	1,934.3	862,696.8
May	(1,745.3)	851,547.9
June	1,859.0	845,733.6
July	671.0	843,937.8
August	(749.6)	837,356.4
September	(3,851.5)	834,784.0
October	(3,368.3)	827,641.5
November	(4,480.6)	828,279.8
December	(13,794.0)	812,494.1
Total	**($4,080.5)**	**$812,494.1**
2000		
January	($12,772.6)	$806,894.8
February	(8,029.6)	809,153.2
March	(8,030.5)	805,857.1
April	(6,596.4)	793,350.5
May	(4,988.1)	781,776.2
June	117.0	796,252.4
July	(186.5)	801,091.8
August	(1,715.0)	806,754.1
September	(3,621.9)	801,663.2
October	(1,971.7)	799,262.1
November	(582.1)	799,036.6
December	(1,385.6)	811,188.5
Total	**($49,763.0)**	**$811,188.5**
2001		
January	$8,971.1	$833,309.2
February	8,854.1	844,512.6
March	7,749.2	852,046.6
April	1,389.8	845,968.1
May	6,305.8	858,351.5
June	2,265.4	860,822.6
July	9,312.3	882,291.3
August	16,713.4	908,315.7
September	7,679.9	909,554.6
October	13,585.1	935,132.8
November	6,917.5	934,084.6
December	(2,039.8)	925,124.0
Total	**$87,703.8**	**$925,124.0**

*Net new cash flow is the dollar value of new sales minus redemptions, combined with net exchanges.

Note: Data for funds that invest in other mutual funds were excluded from the series.

An Overview: Sales, Redemptions, and Net Sales of Equity, Hybrid, and Bond Funds

(millions of dollars)

Year	Sales	Redemptions	Net Sales
1970	$4,625.8	$2,987.6	$1,638.2
1971	5,147.2	4,750.2	397.0
1972	4,892.5	6,562.9	(1,670.4)
1973	4,359.3	5,651.1	(1,291.8)
1974	3,091.5	3,380.9	(289.4)
1975	3,307.2	3,686.3	(379.1)
1976	4,360.5	6,801.2	(2,440.7)
1977	6,399.6	6,026.0	373.6
1978	6,705.3	7,232.4	(527.1)
1979	6,826.1	8,005.0	(1,178.9)
1980	9,993.7	8,200.0	1,793.7
1981	9,710.4	7,470.4	2,240.0
1982	15,738.3	7,571.8	8,166.5
1983	40,325.1	14,677.6	25,647.5
1984	45,857.6	20,030.2	25,827.4
1985	114,238.0	33,814.2	80,423.8
1986	215,345.6	66,988.5	148,357.1
1987	190,214.0	116,076.1	74,137.9
1988	95,114.0	92,326.2	2,787.8
1989	125,336.5	91,526.0	33,810.5
1990	149,091.0	98,065.2	51,025.8
1991	236,340.6	116,582.4	119,758.2
1992	363,155.9	165,303.0	197,852.9
1993	509,885.9	230,972.4	278,913.5
1994	472,417.5	329,218.2	143,199.3
1995	475,408.2	312,894.8	162,513.4
1996	680,905.7	397,430.2	283,475.5
1997	869,025.9	541,192.5	327,833.4
1998	1,057,822.7	747,680.4	310,142.3
1999	1,273,620.9	1,021,188.8	252,432.1
2000	1,630,482.7	1,330,236.9	300,245.8
2001	1,383,050.1	1,176,891.1	206,159.0

Note: The data contain a series break beginning in 1984. All funds were reclassified in 1984 and a separate category was created for hybrid funds. At the same time, data for funds that invest in other mutual funds were excluded from the series.

Sales of Equity, Hybrid, and Bond Funds
by Investment Objective
(millions of dollars)

	1999	2000	2001
Total Sales	**$1,273,620.9**	**$1,630,482.7**	**$1,383,050.1**
Aggressive Growth	$153,230.3	$290,294.8	$191,069.1
Growth	294,832.0	365,277.1	249,664.2
Sector	62,648.9	121,515.3	45,867.8
World Equity–Emerging Markets	7,308.1	11,628.1	10,283.9
World Equity–Global	47,807.3	85,533.8	51,528.1
World Equity–International	108,132.8	210,838.6	172,054.9
World Equity–Regional	22,786.6	27,041.3	16,808.9
Growth and Income	227,631.8	213,817.7	210,521.9
Income Equity	21,634.5	20,478.9	25,491.2
Total Equity Funds	**$946,012.3**	**$1,346,425.6**	**$973,290.0**
Asset Allocation	$6,906.7	$6,962.8	$7,351.3
Balanced	42,799.9	39,993.1	44,164.7
Flexible Portfolio	17,639.2	13,714.5	16,296.1
Income–Mixed	11,902.0	6,956.0	11,448.8
Total Hybrid Funds	**$79,247.8**	**$67,626.4**	**$79,260.9**
Corporate Bond–General	$9,704.6	$8,825.4	$10,882.0
Corporate Bond–Intermediate-Term	25,336.9	17,230.8	25,196.4
Corporate Bond–Short-Term	22,756.6	23,556.7	30,609.6
High-Yield Bond	39,171.9	29,395.9	39,873.2
World Bond–Global General	3,495.0	3,724.6	4,306.9
World Bond–Global Short-Term	1,576.7	1,367.5	952.7
World Bond–Other	1,385.6	1,628.1	1,551.1
Government Bond–General	10,536.6	9,043.1	17,000.7
Government Bond–Intermediate-Term	8,895.3	6,382.5	10,457.8
Government Bond–Short-Term	8,987.0	6,685.2	14,123.1
Government Bond–Mortgage-Backed	15,368.2	9,854.4	27,280.6
Strategic Income	42,749.0	50,310.9	84,723.4
State Municipal Bond–General	23,319.0	17,803.2	26,023.9
State Municipal Bond–Short-Term	3,104.7	2,607.9	2,998.1
National Municipal Bond–General	20,604.0	18,337.5	23,132.0
National Municipal Bond–Short-Term	11,369.7	9,677.0	11,387.7
Total Bond Funds	**$248,360.8**	**$216,430.7**	**$330,499.2**

Note: Data for funds that invest in other mutual funds were excluded from the series.

Reinvested Dividends of Equity, Hybrid, and Bond Funds by Investment Objective

(millions of dollars)

	1999	2000	2001
Total Reinvested Dividends	**$69,972.6**	**$66,276.2**	**$62,313.8**
Aggressive Growth	$1,828.2	$1,448.6	$839.9
Growth	6,451.3	4,826.7	2,746.4
Sector	1,413.2	1,379.5	1,139.3
World Equity–Emerging Markets	86.1	110.6	118.4
World Equity–Global	1,732.2	1,785.7	1,303.3
World Equity–International	2,248.0	2,617.0	1,882.7
World Equity–Regional	298.8	248.0	242.7
Growth and Income	10,739.4	10,166.6	9,795.1
Income Equity	2,534.7	2,006.8	2,022.3
Total Equity Funds	**$27,331.9**	**$24,589.5**	**$20,090.1**
Asset Allocation	$1,077.4	$800.8	$761.6
Balanced	4,846.8	4,262.8	4,188.7
Flexible Portfolio	2,025.3	2,124.5	2,006.9
Income–Mixed	2,796.9	2,088.2	2,010.5
Total Hybrid Funds	**$10,746.4**	**$9,276.3**	**$8,967.7**
Corporate Bond–General	$1,121.8	$1,130.6	$1,078.9
Corporate Bond–Intermediate-Term	3,291.5	2,494.0	2,605.3
Corporate Bond–Short-Term	1,876.2	2,225.4	2,138.2
High-Yield Bond	6,812.0	6,225.3	6,126.2
World Bond–Global General	479.0	412.2	384.3
World Bond–Global Short-Term	173.5	104.3	93.7
World Bond–Other	184.7	292.3	205.3
Government Bond–General	1,457.3	1,292.1	1,427.1
Government Bond–Intermediate-Term	907.2	923.9	966.6
Government Bond–Short-Term	783.4	743.7	652.2
Government Bond–Mortgage-Backed	2,500.8	2,556.0	2,636.5
Strategic Income	4,377.0	6,604.7	7,442.6
State Municipal Bond–General	3,276.5	3,107.9	3,164.9
State Municipal Bond–Short-Term	215.9	151.0	155.8
National Municipal Bond–General	3,536.9	3,479.3	3,537.0
National Municipal Bond–Short-Term	900.6	667.7	641.4
Total Bond Funds	**$31,894.3**	**$32,410.4**	**$33,256.0**

Note: Data for funds that invest in other mutual funds were excluded from the series.

Sales Less Reinvested Dividends of Equity, Hybrid, and Bond Funds by Investment Objective

(millions of dollars)

	1999	2000	2001
Total New Sales	$1,203,648.3	$1,564,206.5	$1,320,736.3
Aggressive Growth	$151,402.1	$288,846.2	$190,229.2
Growth	288,380.7	360,450.4	246,917.8
Sector	61,235.7	120,135.8	44,728.5
World Equity–Emerging Markets	7,222.0	11,517.5	10,165.5
World Equity–Global	46,075.1	83,748.1	50,224.8
World Equity–International	105,884.8	208,221.6	170,172.2
World Equity–Regional	22,487.8	26,793.3	16,566.2
Growth and Income	216,892.4	203,651.1	200,726.8
Income Equity	19,099.8	18,472.1	23,468.9
Total Equity Funds	$918,680.4	$1,321,836.1	$953,199.9
Asset Allocation	$5,829.3	$6,162.0	$6,589.7
Balanced	37,953.1	35,730.3	39,976.0
Flexible Portfolio	15,613.9	11,590.0	14,289.2
Income–Mixed	9,105.1	4,867.8	9,438.3
Total Hybrid Funds	$68,501.4	$58,350.1	$70,293.2
Corporate Bond–General	$8,582.8	$7,694.8	$9,803.1
Corporate Bond–Intermediate-Term	22,045.4	14,736.8	22,591.1
Corporate Bond–Short-Term	20,880.4	21,331.3	28,471.4
High-Yield Bond	32,359.9	23,170.6	33,747.0
World Bond–Global General	3,016.0	3,312.4	3,922.6
World Bond–Global Short-Term	1,403.2	1,263.2	859.0
World Bond–Other	1,200.9	1,335.8	1,345.8
Government Bond–General	9,079.3	7,751.0	15,573.6
Government Bond–Intermediate-Term	7,988.1	5,458.6	9,491.2
Government Bond–Short-Term	8,203.6	5,941.5	13,470.9
Government Bond–Mortgage-Backed	12,867.4	7,298.4	24,644.1
Strategic Income	38,372.0	43,706.2	77,280.8
State Municipal Bond–General	20,042.5	14,695.3	22,859.0
State Municipal Bond–Short-Term	2,888.8	2,456.9	2,842.3
National Municipal Bond–General	17,067.1	14,858.2	19,595.0
National Municipal Bond–Short-Term	10,469.1	9,009.3	10,746.3
Total Bond Funds	$216,466.5	$184,020.3	$297,243.2

Note: Data for funds that invest in other mutual funds were excluded from the series.

Equity, Hybrid, and Bond Fund Distributions to Shareholders

(millions of dollars)

Year	Total	Dividend Distributions			Total	Capital Gain Distributions		
		Equity Funds	Hybrid Funds	Bond Funds		Equity Funds	Hybrid Funds	Bond Funds
1985	$12,719.3	$3,229.0	$1,098.1	$8,392.2	$4,894.5	$3,699.3	$738.5	$456.7
1986	22,689.3	6,328.3	1,499.3	14,861.7	17,660.9	13,942.4	1,240.1	2,478.4
1987	31,707.9	7,246.4	1,933.6	22,527.9	22,925.6	18,602.8	1,604.5	2,718.3
1988	31,965.9	6,554.1	1,872.5	23,539.3	6,353.5	4,785.3	620.2	948.0
1989	34,102.4	10,235.1	2,164.9	21,702.4	14,765.8	12,664.7	539.5	1,561.6
1990	33,156.0	8,787.4	2,350.3	22,018.3	8,017.2	6,832.6	442.9	741.7
1991	35,145.0	9,007.0	2,337.1	23,800.9	13,917.2	11,961.0	861.0	1,095.2
1992	58,608.3	17,022.8	4,483.4	37,102.1	22,088.6	17,294.4	1,488.3	3,305.9
1993	73,177.6	20,230.0	6,810.2	46,137.4	35,904.6	27,704.8	3,495.8	4,704.0
1994	61,320.5	17,336.9	6,897.6	37,086.0	29,825.4	26,431.7	2,412.6	981.1
1995	67,230.6	22,567.2	9,053.5	35,610.1	54,274.5	50,203.9	3,346.8	723.8
1996	73,291.6	25,062.5	9,851.6	38,377.5	100,508.3	88,211.8	10,845.7	1,450.8
1997	79,896.2	27,971.2	11,606.7	40,318.3	183,385.8	161,365.3	19,079.9	2,940.6
1998	81,013.8	25,499.0	11,451.8	44,063.0	164,991.1	138,687.0	21,565.1	4,739.0
1999	95,443.1	32,543.8	13,100.6	49,798.7	237,624.7	219,484.5	16,841.0	1,299.2
2000	88,213.9	27,987.4	10,681.1	49,545.4	325,872.4	307,618.0	17,807.9	446.5
2001	82,975.8	22,325.5	10,169.4	50,480.9	68,894.0	60,718.4	5,754.6	2,421.0

Note: Data for funds that invest in other mutual funds were excluded from the series.

Annual Redemption Rate for Equity, Hybrid, and Bond Funds
(millions of dollars)

Year	Average Total Net Assets	Redemptions	Redemption Rate
1970	$47,954	$2,988	6.2%
1971	51,332	4,750	9.3
1972	57,438	6,563	11.4
1973	53,175	5,651	10.6
1974	40,290	3,381	8.4
1975	38,120	3,686	9.7
1976	44,880	6,801	15.2
1977	46,316	6,026	13.0
1978	45,014	7,232	16.1
1979	46,980	8,005	17.0
1980	53,690	8,200	15.3
1981	56,803	7,470	13.2
1982	66,024	7,572	11.5
1983	95,220	14,678	15.4
1984	125,983	20,030	15.9
1985	201,366	33,814	16.8
1986	344,426	66,989	19.4
1987	458,405	116,076	25.3
1988	469,801	92,326	19.7
1989	519,432	91,526	17.6
1990	550,371	98,065	17.8
1991	736,207	116,582	15.8
1992	981,037	165,303	16.8
1993	1,316,011	230,972	17.6
1994	1,555,755	329,218	21.2
1995	1,807,283	312,895	17.3
1996	2,378,390	397,430	16.7
1997	3,073,865	541,193	17.6
1998	3,814,974	747,680	19.6
1999	4,759,809	1,021,189	21.5
2000	5,116,828	1,330,237	26.0
2001	4,985,677	1,176,891	23.6

Note: "Average Total Net Assets" are an average of values at the beginning of the year and at the end of the year. The redemption rate is the dollar redemption volume as a percent of average assets. The data contain a series break beginning in 1984. All funds were reclassified in 1984 and a separate category was created for hybrid funds. At the same time, data for funds that invest in other mutual funds were excluded from the series.

Redemptions of Equity, Hybrid, and Bond Funds
by Investment Objective
(millions of dollars)

	1999	2000	2001
Total Redemptions	$1,021,188.8	$1,330,236.9	$1,176,891.1
Aggressive Growth	$125,184.3	$186,842.9	$168,679.9
Growth	206,029.4	263,494.6	228,247.2
Sector	36,468.6	71,114.5	49,469.2
World Equity–Emerging Markets	6,816.1	11,259.4	11,093.4
World Equity–Global	42,334.2	63,250.2	56,286.4
World Equity–International	100,680.6	179,235.7	173,045.6
World Equity–Regional	21,406.7	28,468.7	18,723.7
Growth and Income	178,907.2	206,563.4	167,234.7
Income Equity	26,325.6	28,343.1	20,139.9
Total Equity Funds	**$744,152.7**	**$1,038,572.5**	**$892,920.0**
Asset Allocation	$9,118.0	$7,958.4	$6,757.6
Balanced	33,914.3	39,401.6	31,577.5
Flexible Portfolio	16,322.7	17,241.7	15,660.3
Income–Mixed	11,712.7	9,908.6	7,042.8
Total Hybrid Funds	**$71,067.7**	**$74,510.3**	**$61,038.2**
Corporate Bond–General	$8,414.6	$8,971.3	$8,415.2
Corporate Bond–Intermediate-Term	17,644.4	16,313.8	19,483.3
Corporate Bond–Short-Term	18,509.8	23,812.4	25,632.2
High-Yield Bond	32,125.4	30,805.3	26,798.9
World Bond–Global General	3,947.8	3,698.2	4,089.6
World Bond–Global Short-Term	1,873.2	1,852.2	1,160.4
World Bond–Other	1,270.3	1,985.7	1,511.8
Government Bond–General	10,324.8	9,857.7	10,606.0
Government Bond–Intermediate-Term	6,669.8	7,176.6	7,179.4
Government Bond–Short-Term	7,339.6	7,196.3	10,332.7
Government Bond–Mortgage-Backed	12,305.0	13,459.6	11,789.5
Strategic Income	28,068.4	38,718.6	50,531.1
State Municipal Bond–General	22,381.3	19,947.7	16,961.4
State Municipal Bond–Short-Term	2,794.9	2,129.4	1,959.4
National Municipal Bond–General	21,286.3	22,395.2	18,153.7
National Municipal Bond–Short-Term	11,012.8	8,834.1	8,328.3
Total Bond Funds	**$205,968.4**	**$217,154.1**	**$222,932.9**

Note: Data for funds that invest in other mutual funds were excluded from the series.

Total Purchases, Total Sales, and Net Purchases of Portfolio Securities by Equity, Hybrid, and Bond Funds
(millions of dollars)

Year	Total Purchases	Total Sales	Net Purchases
1970	$20,405.0	$18,588.5	$1,816.5
1971	25,360.2	24,793.8	566.4
1972	24,467.6	25,823.6	(1,356.0)
1973	19,706.6	21,903.0	(2,196.4)
1974	12,299.7	12,213.5	86.2
1975	15,396.9	15,511.4	(114.5)
1976	15,348.2	16,881.2	(1,533.0)
1977	18,168.0	19,420.7	(1,252.7)
1978	20,945.6	23,069.7	(2,124.1)
1979	22,412.1	23,702.5	(1,290.4)
1980	32,987.2	32,080.6	906.6
1981	36,161.7	33,709.2	2,452.5
1982	55,682.0	47,920.7	7,761.3
1983	93,009.5	71,466.5	21,543.0
1984	119,272.6	98,934.5	20,338.1
1985	259,496.1	186,985.2	72,510.9
1986	500,596.6	365,087.4	135,509.2
1987	530,600.7	485,270.9	45,329.8
1988	410,509.2	421,223.7	(10,714.5)
1989	471,744.1	445,453.3	26,290.8
1990	554,719.8	505,779.6	48,940.2
1991	735,674.4	608,111.1	127,563.3
1992	949,366.0	758,475.0	190,891.0
1993	1,335,505.6	1,060,360.3	275,145.3
1994	1,433,738.7	1,329,324.2	104,414.5
1995	1,550,510.3	1,400,701.8	149,808.5
1996	2,018,253.2	1,736,883.7	281,369.5
1997	2,384,639.4	2,108,980.6	275,658.8
1998	2,861,561.9	2,560,074.4	301,487.5
1999	3,437,179.7	3,224,301.2	212,878.5
2000	4,923,152.2	4,698,519.0	224,633.2
2001	4,692,997.7	4,397,643.6	295,354.1

Note: The data contain a series break beginning in 1984. All funds were reclassified in 1984 and a separate category was created for hybrid funds. At the same time, data for funds that invest in other mutual funds were excluded from the series.

Total Purchases, Total Sales, and Net Purchases of Common Stocks by Equity, Hybrid, and Bond Funds
(millions of dollars)

Year	Total Purchases	Total Sales	Net Purchases
1970	$17,127.6	$15,900.8	$1,226.8
1971	21,557.7	21,175.1	382.6
1972	20,943.5	22,552.8	(1,609.3)
1973	15,560.7	17,504.4	(1,943.7)
1974	9,085.3	9,372.1	(286.8)
1975	10,948.7	11,902.3	(953.6)
1976	10,729.1	13,278.3	(2,549.2)
1977	8,704.7	12,211.3	(3,506.6)
1978	12,832.9	14,454.7	(1,621.8)
1979	13,089.0	15,923.0	(2,834.0)
1980	19,893.8	21,799.9	(1,906.1)
1981	20,859.7	21,278.3	(418.6)
1982	27,397.2	24,939.6	2,457.6
1983	54,581.7	40,813.9	13,767.8
1984	56,588.1	50,899.9	5,688.2
1985	80,719.0	72,577.4	8,141.6
1986	134,446.4	118,025.7	16,420.7
1987	198,859.3	176,003.9	22,855.4
1988	112,742.3	128,815.2	(16,072.9)
1989	142,770.9	141,694.3	1,076.6
1990	166,397.6	146,580.2	19,817.4
1991	250,288.7	209,275.8	41,012.9
1992	327,517.7	261,857.2	65,660.6
1993	506,712.7	380,855.2	125,857.5
1994	628,667.8	512,346.4	116,321.4
1995	790,016.7	686,756.2	103,260.5
1996	1,151,262.3	927,265.9	223,996.4
1997	1,457,384.4	1,268,983.5	188,400.9
1998	1,762,565.3	1,597,310.7	165,254.6
1999	2,262,505.4	2,088,543.7	173,961.7
2000	3,560,898.8	3,330,713.7	230,185.1
2001	2,740,505.5	2,613,332.7	127,172.8

Note: The data contain a series break beginning in 1984. All funds were reclassified in 1984 and a separate category was created for hybrid funds. At the same time, data for funds that invest in other mutual funds were excluded from the series.

Total Purchases, Total Sales, and Net Purchases of Securities Other Than Common Stocks by Equity, Hybrid, and Bond Funds
(millions of dollars)

Year	Total Purchases	Total Sales	Net Purchases
1970	$3,277.4	$2,687.7	$589.7
1971	3,802.5	3,618.7	183.8
1972	3,524.1	3,270.8	253.3
1973	4,145.9	4,398.6	(252.7)
1974	3,214.4	2,841.4	373.0
1975	4,448.2	3,609.1	839.1
1976	4,619.1	3,602.9	1,016.2
1977	9,463.3	7,209.4	2,253.9
1978	8,112.7	8,615.0	(502.3)
1979	9,323.1	7,779.5	1,543.6
1980	13,093.4	10,280.7	2,812.7
1981	15,302.0	12,430.9	2,871.1
1982	28,284.8	22,981.1	5,303.7
1983	38,427.8	30,652.6	7,775.2
1984	62,684.5	48,034.6	14,649.9
1985	178,777.1	114,407.8	64,369.3
1986	366,150.2	247,061.7	119,088.5
1987	331,741.4	309,267.0	22,474.4
1988	297,766.9	292,408.5	5,358.3
1989	328,973.2	303,759.0	25,214.2
1990	388,322.2	359,199.4	29,122.8
1991	485,385.7	398,835.3	86,550.4
1992	621,848.3	496,617.8	125,230.5
1993	828,792.9	679,505.1	149,287.7
1994	805,070.9	816,977.8	(11,906.9)
1995	760,493.6	713,945.6	46,548.0
1996	867,990.9	809,617.8	57,373.1
1997	927,255.0	839,997.1	87,257.9
1998	1,098,996.6	962,763.7	136,232.9
1999	1,174,674.3	1,135,757.5	38,916.8
2000	1,362,253.4	1,367,805.3	(5,551.9)
2001	1,952,492.2	1,784,310.9	168,181.3

Note: The data contain a series break beginning in 1984. All funds were reclassified in 1984 and a separate category was created for hybrid funds. At the same time, data for funds that invest in other mutual funds were excluded from the series.

Portfolio Purchases by Investment Objective

(millions of dollars)

	All Securities		Common Stock Only	
	2000	2001	2000	2001
Total	$4,923,152.2	$4,692,997.7	$3,560,898.8	$2,740,505.5
Aggressive Growth	$869,293.9	$660,591.1	$848,470.4	$641,849.6
Growth	1,193,023.6	905,094.5	1,165,669.2	876,585.8
Sector	290,744.4	179,844.4	285,960.4	172,669.9
World Equity–Emerging Markets	20,440.5	14,534.8	17,774.0	12,865.2
World Equity–Global	225,114.0	149,801.1	208,494.2	137,084.6
World Equity–International	280,807.3	195,132.0	267,088.3	179,034.6
World Equity–Regional	32,902.6	23,725.7	31,807.6	21,678.8
Growth and Income	555,131.0	526,917.8	512,050.8	475,721.8
Income Equity	70,116.5	78,473.0	59,658.4	61,739.5
Total Equity Funds	**$3,537,573.8**	**$2,734,114.4**	**$3,396,973.3**	**$2,579,229.8**
Asset Allocation	$43,273.2	$45,434.1	$28,077.8	$25,955.7
Balanced	163,003.1	197,169.1	78,919.5	81,199.1
Flexible Portfolio	74,263.9	80,378.2	41,642.4	37,165.5
Income–Mixed	37,122.6	39,101.7	7,488.6	8,961.3
Total Hybrid Funds	**$317,662.8**	**$362,083.1**	**$156,128.3**	**$153,281.6**
Corporate Bond–General	$43,286.5	$85,120.1	$101.5	$514.0
Corporate Bond– Intermediate-Term	98,468.1	159,814.4	1,133.4	1,227.8
Corporate Bond–Short-Term	37,944.4	65,319.2	912.6	431.6
High-Yield Bond	62,039.0	84,146.0	3,023.0	2,701.5
World Bond–Global General	25,720.1	25,880.1	935.2	507.0
World Bond–Global Short-Term	5,379.1	3,382.6	51.2	130.4
World Bond–Other	13,123.4	11,729.0	321.1	375.4
Government Bond–General	82,675.7	129,992.5	–	–
Government Bond– Intermediate-Term	30,431.3	48,778.1	–	–
Government Bond–Short-Term	33,672.4	46,329.8	–	–
Government Bond– Mortgage-Backed	139,384.3	145,872.6	–	–
Strategic Income	391,822.0	652,908.0	1,319.2	2,106.4
State Municipal Bond–General	37,001.9	51,516.6	–	–
State Municipal Bond–Short-Term	2,976.2	5,582.2	–	–
National Municipal Bond–General	48,223.4	60,161.3	–	–
National Municipal Bond– Short-Term	15,767.8	20,267.7	–	–
Total Bond Funds	**$1,067,915.6**	**$1,596,800.2**	**$7,797.2**	**$7,994.1**

Note: Data for funds that invest in other mutual funds were excluded from the series.

Portfolio Sales by Investment Objective
(millions of dollars)

	All Securities		Common Stock Only	
	2000	2001	2000	2001
Total	$4,698,519.0	$4,397,643.6	$3,330,713.7	$2,613,332.7
Aggressive Growth	$766,923.1	$620,728.4	$747,582.3	$602,280.0
Growth	1,088,931.9	879,763.7	1,060,010.5	849,158.9
Sector	237,706.8	179,975.5	233,586.2	172,809.3
World Equity–Emerging Markets	20,748.3	14,958.7	18,061.5	13,027.2
World Equity–Global	202,307.3	149,605.0	188,436.1	134,882.5
World Equity–International	255,458.6	191,680.1	241,815.7	175,482.4
World Equity–Regional	36,775.9	26,743.8	35,688.3	24,848.8
Growth and Income	587,432.1	484,478.7	548,775.7	442,922.0
Income Equity	90,096.3	70,960.9	78,827.6	56,447.6
Total Equity Funds	**$3,286,380.3**	**$2,618,894.8**	**$3,152,783.9**	**$2,471,858.7**
Asset Allocation	$45,194.9	$44,365.6	$30,095.2	$24,677.5
Balanced	167,878.5	180,848.2	84,383.7	66,496.0
Flexible Portfolio	80,565.4	79,438.4	42,881.8	33,339.4
Income–Mixed	45,556.9	34,456.8	11,189.2	8,479.3
Total Hybrid Funds	**$339,195.7**	**$339,109.0**	**$168,549.9**	**$132,992.2**
Corporate Bond–General	$42,899.7	$80,017.4	$113.3	$406.7
Corporate Bond– Intermediate-Term	97,780.7	152,274.6	1,186.6	1,127.0
Corporate Bond–Short-Term	36,060.3	57,127.5	1,871.5	424.2
High-Yield Bond	72,331.1	70,210.8	3,350.4	3,167.8
World Bond–Global General	25,360.0	25,722.9	938.7	643.3
World Bond–Global Short-Term	5,741.3	3,573.6	45.2	120.5
World Bond–Other	13,655.8	11,695.1	339.6	311.6
Government Bond–General	83,666.8	121,570.5	–	–
Government Bond– Intermediate-Term	31,282.7	43,363.3	–	–
Government Bond–Short-Term	36,802.4	39,708.4	–	–
Government Bond– Mortgage-Backed	140,585.8	119,263.9	–	–
Strategic Income	373,365.5	598,237.9	1,534.6	2,280.7
State Municipal Bond–General	40,723.5	42,161.3	–	–
State Municipal Bond–Short-Term	3,375.6	4,602.3	–	–
National Municipal Bond–General	53,464.7	53,847.0	–	–
National Municipal Bond– Short-Term	15,847.1	16,263.3	–	–
Total Bond Funds	**$1,072,943.0**	**$1,439,639.8**	**$9,379.9**	**$8,481.8**

Note: Data for funds that invest in other mutual funds were excluded from the series.

Section Three: U.S. Industry Short-Term Funds

Total Short-Term Funds

(millions of dollars)

Year	Total Sales	Total Redemptions	Net Sales	Net New Cash Flow*	Dividend Distributions	Number of Funds	Total Accounts Outstanding	Total Net Assets
1980	$237,427.7	$207,877.7	$29,550.0	$24,022.7	$7,765.7	106	4,762,103	$76,361.3
1981	462,422.6	354,972.1	107,450.5	91,143.7	18,573.3	179	10,323,466	186,158.2
1982	611,202.9	580,778.4	30,424.5	9,184.1	21,980.0	318	13,258,143	219,837.5
1983	507,447.0	551,151.3	(43,704.3)	(55,664.9)	13,782.3	373	12,539,688	179,386.5
1984	634,228.0	586,990.5	47,237.5	33,040.5	16,434.9	425	13,844,697	233,553.6
1985	839,498.9	831,065.6	8,433.3	(8,940.9)	15,707.7	460	14,934,631	243,802.4
1986	989,816.0	948,641.4	41,174.7	26,465.1	14,832.1	487	16,313,148	292,151.6
1987	1,060,949.2	1,062,520.2	(1,571.0)	(5,189.0)	15,654.0	543	17,674,790	316,096.1
1988	1,081,695.1	1,074,340.3	7,355.0	(8,961.9)	21,618.1	610	18,569,817	337,953.6
1989	1,319,453.1	1,235,527.0	83,926.1	55,703.4	28,618.8	673	21,314,228	428,093.3
1990	1,415,701.3	1,372,725.3	42,976.1	23,219.6	30,257.9	741	22,968,817	498,341.4
1991	1,800,758.0	1,763,106.3	37,651.8	5,499.0	28,604.3	820	23,556,000	542,441.7
1992	2,386,288.2	2,382,975.9	3,312.4	(16,288.9)	20,279.7	864	23,647,186	546,194.6
1993	2,677,539.6	2,673,464.4	4,075.1	(14,110.2)	18,991.3	920	23,585,329	565,319.1
1994	2,603,333.9	2,598,992.9	4,341.0	8,766.9	23,736.6	963	25,378,671	611,004.5
1995	3,125,209.0	3,001,928.0	123,281.0	89,411.1	37,037.7	997	30,136,777	753,017.7
1996	3,990,530.5	3,868,771.7	121,758.9	89,421.8	42,554.8	988	32,199,937	901,807.0
1997	4,930,584.6	4,782,897.7	147,686.9	102,069.4	48,842.6	1,013	35,624,081	1,058,885.7
1998	6,172,574.9	5,901,591.2	270,983.4	235,335.2	57,375.5	1,026	38,847,345	1,351,678.2
1999	7,769,960.2	7,540,911.9	229,048.6	193,630.4	69,004.0	1,045	43,615,576	1,613,145.5
2000	9,478,951.7	9,255,974.5	222,977.1	159,635.6	98,218.6	1,039	48,138,495	1,845,280.7
2001	11,483,164.5	11,065,103.8	418,060.7	375,647.3	79,308.9	1,015	47,236,474	2,285,347.9

*Net new cash flow is the dollar value of new sales minus redemptions, combined with net exchanges.

Note: Data for funds that invest in other mutual funds were excluded from the series.

An Overview: Taxable Money Market Funds
(millions of dollars)

Year	Total Sales	Total Redemptions	Net Sales	Net New Cash Flow*	Dividend Distributions	Number of Funds	Total Accounts Outstanding	Average Maturity (days)	Total Net Assets
1980	$232,172.8	$204,068.5	$28,104.3	$22,527.6	$7,665.7	96	4,745,572	24	$74,447.7
1981	451,889.5	346,701.5	105,188.0	88,939.7	18,473.3	159	10,282,095	34	181,910.4
1982	581,758.9	559,581.1	22,177.8	1,704.2	21,680.0	281	13,101,347	37	206,607.5
1983	462,978.7	508,729.9	(45,751.2)	(57,437.5)	13,182.3	307	12,276,639	37	162,549.5
1984	571,959.3	531,050.9	40,908.4	29,163.5	15,434.9	329	13,556,180	43	209,731.9
1985	730,073.8	732,343.0	(2,269.1)	(15,884.1)	14,107.7	348	14,435,386	42	207,535.3
1986	792,349.1	776,303.2	16,045.9	9,028.8	12,432.1	360	15,653,595	45	228,345.8
1987	869,099.2	865,668.4	3,430.7	13,054.6	12,832.9	389	16,832,666	34	254,676.4
1988	903,425.9	899,397.3	4,028.6	(1,512.4)	17,976.0	434	17,630,528	31	272,293.3
1989	1,134,647.8	1,055,142.4	79,505.4	62,537.5	24,682.9	470	20,173,265	40	358,719.2
1990	1,218,935.9	1,183,085.9	35,850.1	17,433.2	26,447.6	506	21,577,559	47	414,733.3
1991	1,569,852.0	1,536,509.6	33,342.4	4,420.8	25,120.9	553	21,863,352	56	452,559.2
1992	2,099,796.8	2,101,420.8	(1,624.0)	(20,468.2)	17,196.9	585	21,770,693	58	451,353.4
1993	2,335,653.0	2,336,939.6	(1,286.7)	(19,122.8)	15,689.5	628	21,586,862	59	461,903.9
1994	2,234,069.0	2,229,036.6	5,032.4	7,932.4	20,500.2	646	23,339,838	38	500,635.5
1995	2,729,117.5	2,617,221.3	111,896.2	82,127.1	32,822.2	674	27,859,258	57	629,985.8
1996	3,523,786.6	3,415,494.5	108,292.1	79,186.0	38,363.9	666	29,907,471	54	761,989.0
1997	4,394,583.3	4,265,341.8	129,241.5	86,649.7	44,109.6	682	32,960,628	55	898,083.1
1998	5,533,565.3	5,289,265.8	244,299.4	212,408.3	52,072.4	685	36,442,150	56	1,163,166.7
1999	7,083,029.5	6,865,682.3	217,347.3	182,795.8	63,107.4	702	41,177,138	49	1,408,731.0
2000	8,690,835.2	8,499,014.5	191,820.7	133,120.3	89,955.8	703	45,479,697	51	1,607,248.2
2001	10,700,522.6	10,313,681.3	386,841.3	349,426.1	73,117.3	689	44,414,701	58	2,012,949.4

*Net new cash flow is the dollar value of new sales minus redemptions, combined with net exchanges.

Note: Data for funds that invest in other mutual funds were excluded from the series.

Section Three: U.S. Industry Short-Term Funds

An Overview: Tax-Exempt Money Market Funds

(millions of dollars)

Year		Total Sales	Total Redemptions	Net Sales	Net New Cash Flow*	Dividend Distributions	Number of Funds	Total Accounts Outstanding	Total Net Assets
1988	National	$158,078.9	$158,087.5	($8.5)	($8,698.5)	$2,990.1	122	754,068	$54,541.8
	State	20,190.3	16,855.5	3,334.9	1,249.0	652.0	54	185,221	11,118.5
1989	National	152,674.0	151,735.4	938.6	(7,468.8)	3,011.1	131	875,626	52,824.7
	State	32,131.3	28,649.2	3,482.1	634.7	924.8	72	265,337	16,549.4
1990	National	155,956.9	153,363.8	2,593.1	1,162.5	2,688.9	133	984,301	59,200.5
	State	40,808.5	36,275.6	4,532.9	4,623.9	1,121.4	102	406,957	24,407.6
1991	National	181,137.9	178,927.1	2,210.9	474.1	2,463.2	141	1,139,741	62,338.0
	State	49,768.1	47,669.6	2,098.5	604.1	1,020.2	126	552,907	27,544.5
1992	National	223,414.2	220,832.0	2,582.3	2,659.5	2,171.5	139	1,120,735	64,863.3
	State	63,077.2	60,723.1	2,354.1	1,519.8	911.3	140	755,758	29,977.9
1993	National	264,844.1	261,686.2	3,157.9	2,753.6	2,024.1	145	1,237,326	70,451.2
	State	77,042.5	74,838.6	2,203.9	2,259.0	1,277.7	147	761,141	32,964.0
1994	National	281,800.3	283,647.0	(1,846.7)	(932.6)	1,810.3	154	1,267,090	73,120.1
	State	87,464.6	86,309.3	1,155.3	1,767.1	1,426.1	163	771,743	37,248.9
1995	National	291,273.2	286,223.2	5,050.0	2,449.7	2,832.0	154	1,377,008	79,227.4
	State	104,818.3	98,483.5	6,334.8	4,834.3	1,383.5	169	900,511	43,804.5
1996	National	340,669.6	334,148.6	6,521.0	4,359.5	2,795.9	155	1,346,220	88,845.7
	State	126,074.3	119,128.6	6,945.8	5,876.3	1,395.0	167	946,246	50,972.3
1997	National	383,863.2	373,233.5	10,629.7	8,939.7	3,059.7	156	1,557,399	100,911.3
	State	152,138.1	144,322.4	7,815.7	6,480.0	1,673.3	175	1,106,054	59,891.3
1998	National	452,774.4	437,679.8	15,094.5	13,100.6	3,446.3	155	1,284,287	117,373.9
	State	186,235.2	174,645.6	11,589.5	9,826.3	1,856.8	186	1,120,908	71,137.6
1999	National	474,581.0	470,076.8	4,504.3	4,545.9	3,709.0	158	1,310,161	125,397.3
	State	212,349.7	205,152.8	7,197.0	6,288.7	2,187.6	185	1,128,277	79,017.2
2000	National	533,975.1	513,076.6	20,898.5	17,868.3	5,255.9	151	1,411,570	145,280.9
	State	254,141.4	243,883.4	10,257.9	8,647.0	3,006.9	185	1,247,228	92,751.6
2001	National	552,860.2	527,933.3	24,926.9	22,649.6	4,077.5	140	1,521,077	174,376.3
	State	229,781.7	223,489.2	6,292.5	3,571.6	2,114.1	186	1,300,696	98,022.2

*Net new cash flow is the dollar value of new sales minus redemptions, combined with net exchanges.

Taxable Money Market Fund Monthly Total Net Assets by Type of Fund
(thousands of dollars)

	Retail	Institutional	Total
1999			
January	$711,589,933	$506,975,354	$1,218,565,287
February	733,309,788	509,849,984	1,243,159,772
March	742,385,570	496,164,575	1,238,550,145
April	733,958,496	495,558,554	1,229,517,050
May	734,019,722	503,198,208	1,237,217,930
June	733,322,421	496,051,955	1,229,374,376
July	744,944,794	505,718,337	1,250,663,131
August	762,679,930	521,860,469	1,284,540,399
September	770,055,213	513,510,718	1,283,565,931
October	774,192,353	549,102,447	1,323,294,800
November	796,891,038	576,770,982	1,373,662,020
December	808,377,229	600,353,771	1,408,731,000
2000			
January	$832,568,272	$612,499,921	$1,445,068,193
February	843,223,145	622,341,486	1,465,564,631
March	866,748,438	608,952,364	1,475,700,802
April	843,038,890	597,328,042	1,440,366,932
May	843,437,961	615,927,596	1,459,365,557
June	828,061,712	615,581,881	1,443,643,593
July	838,105,705	638,841,591	1,476,947,296
August	844,091,362	662,344,588	1,506,435,950
September	845,498,188	661,843,727	1,507,341,915
October	849,952,862	684,206,427	1,534,159,289
November	871,577,916	716,635,580	1,588,213,496
December	879,526,309	727,721,910	1,607,248,219
2001			
January	$903,052,211	$811,820,187	$1,714,872,398
February	924,263,455	846,468,599	1,770,732,054
March	956,542,666	829,873,968	1,786,416,634
April	929,332,097	862,848,493	1,792,180,590
May	917,775,910	906,094,208	1,823,870,118
June	908,804,779	895,867,981	1,804,672,760
July	921,796,957	893,279,007	1,815,075,964
August	929,633,516	917,065,554	1,846,699,070
September	950,859,457	951,903,897	1,902,763,354
October	954,755,053	1,019,606,010	1,974,361,063
November	950,797,066	1,081,914,608	2,032,711,674
December	941,486,242	1,071,463,190	2,012,949,432

Note: Data for funds that invest in other mutual funds were excluded from the series.

Taxable Money Market Fund
Shareholder Accounts by Type of Fund

	Retail	Institutional	Total
1999			
January	33,881,111	3,311,141	37,192,252
February	34,408,994	3,311,180	37,720,174
March	34,480,851	3,324,430	37,805,281
April	34,854,790	3,398,872	38,253,662
May	35,431,038	3,406,439	38,837,477
June	35,620,703	3,512,607	39,133,310
July	36,029,205	3,928,663	39,957,868
August	36,353,831	4,040,334	40,394,165
September	36,238,145	4,115,706	40,353,851
October	36,575,565	4,253,907	40,829,472
November	37,147,411	4,241,708	41,389,119
December	37,008,204	4,168,934	41,177,138
2000			
January	37,229,650	3,866,471	41,096,121
February	37,582,763	3,798,987	41,381,750
March	39,045,555	3,786,889	42,832,444
April	39,523,668	3,465,147	42,988,815
May	39,684,064	3,935,315	43,619,379
June	38,773,943	3,796,364	42,570,307
July	38,806,874	3,728,590	42,535,464
August	38,917,885	3,757,663	42,675,548
September	40,799,576	4,192,271	44,991,847
October	40,651,349	4,240,106	44,891,455
November	41,234,620	4,334,857	45,569,477
December	41,159,614	4,320,083	45,479,697
2001			
January	41,447,999	4,508,329	45,956,328
February	41,882,816	4,650,059	46,532,875
March	42,257,917	4,795,690	47,053,607
April	41,830,688	4,751,895	46,582,583
May	42,021,649	4,849,741	46,871,390
June	41,772,706	4,817,715	46,590,421
July	40,402,682	4,904,139	45,306,821
August	40,464,924	4,995,550	45,460,474
September	38,797,825	5,045,523	43,843,348
October	39,399,975	5,072,282	44,472,257
November	40,136,819	5,082,670	45,219,489
December	39,347,593	5,067,108	44,414,701

Note: Data for funds that invest in other mutual funds were excluded from the series.

Taxable Money Market Fund Asset Composition

(millions of dollars)

	1995	1996	1997	1998	1999	2000	2001
Total Net Assets	**$629,985.8**	**$761,989.0**	**$898,083.1**	**$1,163,166.7**	**$1,408,731.0**	**$1,607,248.2**	**$2,012,949.4**
U.S. Treasury Bills	42,280.8	42,195.0	40,955.2	48,115.7	60,054.6	54,515.4	93,450.2
Other Treasury Securities	29,347.6	49,644.1	47,934.1	62,005.4	46,311.1	37,843.0	45,345.7
U.S. Securities	92,752.0	104,189.2	97,804.1	176,043.0	195,734.0	189,095.7	325,656.1
Repurchase Agreements	89,316.2	105,710.6	128,901.5	141,710.8	143,975.3	186,890.2	232,186.8
Certificates of Deposits	39,898.6	69,316.8	95,565.7	111,908.4	138,984.6	122,576.9	195,809.3
Eurodollar CDs	20,066.2	23,569.3	23,951.9	30,713.8	42,095.9	93,026.8	127,034.9
Commercial Paper	237,121.9	276,801.4	339,501.0	420,975.0	535,288.5	619,722.7	649,636.4
Bank Notes	16,727.7	12,398.3	21,017.4	33,668.5	33,828.2	46,120.5	25,342.4
Bankers Acceptances	3,059.6	2,619.9	3,472.6	2,860.5	2,884.3	1,782.5	3,850.5
Corporate Notes*	—	—	—	50,255.0	94,010.8	119,175.6	141,353.8
Cash Reserves	(3,596.0)	(1,159.2)	1,479.5	(1,046.9)	(3,392.7)	2,276.1	4,664.8
Other Assets	63,011.2	76,703.6	97,500.1	85,957.5	118,956.4	134,222.8	168,618.5
Average Maturity (days)	57	54	55	56	49	51	58
Number of Funds	674	666	682	685	702	703	689

*Prior to 1998, corporate notes are included in the "Other Assets" category.

Note: Data for funds that invest in other mutual funds were excluded from the series.

Sales Due to Exchanges by Investment Objective
(millions of dollars)

	1999	2000	2001
Total	**$949,940.4**	**$1,149,752.6**	**$797,339.5**
Aggressive Growth	$122,117.6	$193,321.2	$107,080.8
Growth	128,962.1	162,318.0	93,336.6
Sector	53,726.9	84,483.8	41,672.4
World Equity–Emerging Markets	3,213.9	5,254.6	1,859.2
World Equity–Global	38,729.1	52,298.9	21,384.8
World Equity–International	53,143.1	75,843.4	41,664.2
World Equity–Regional	16,355.9	15,680.2	10,798.8
Growth and Income	68,447.5	57,929.7	51,260.2
Income Equity	7,636.4	6,914.1	8,431.5
Total Equity Funds	**$492,332.5**	**$654,043.9**	**$377,488.5**
Asset Allocation	$2,467.2	$2,935.0	$4,611.5
Balanced	8,078.0	6,630.2	8,814.1
Flexible Portfolio	2,274.4	2,340.7	1,983.4
Income–Mixed	1,504.5	1,567.3	2,070.6
Total Hybrid Funds	**$14,324.1**	**$13,473.2**	**$17,479.6**
Corporate Bond–General	$2,180.5	$2,023.2	$3,343.7
Corporate Bond–Intermediate-Term	5,626.1	3,461.9	6,840.0
Corporate Bond–Short-Term	5,698.3	3,708.3	7,501.9
High-Yield Bond	13,000.2	10,268.3	11,093.0
World Bond–Global General	972.7	959.6	714.7
World Bond–Global Short-Term	104.6	93.2	107.7
World Bond–Other	289.4	280.0	339.9
Government Bond–General	5,785.6	3,615.2	8,308.4
Government Bond–Intermediate-Term	4,262.3	2,850.9	5,677.7
Government Bond–Short-Term	5,243.5	3,016.3	4,349.1
Government Bond–Mortgage-Backed	7,850.2	7,232.9	8,359.3
Strategic Income	6,601.6	8,161.0	16,216.4
State Municipal Bond–General	6,383.5	5,121.1	5,086.2
State Municipal Bond–Short-Term	601.0	187.7	280.4
National Municipal Bond–General	14,004.5	8,992.3	11,238.1
National Municipal Bond–Short-Term	3,051.1	1,873.0	2,428.1
Total Bond Funds	**$81,655.1**	**$61,844.9**	**$91,884.6**
Taxable Money Market–Government	$50,027.5	$45,305.9	$40,665.9
Taxable Money Market– Non-Government	289,513.4	356,477.7	252,639.9
National Tax-Exempt Money Market	16,250.5	12,403.7	11,030.2
State Tax-Exempt Money Market	5,837.3	6,203.3	6,150.8
Total Money Market Funds	**$361,628.7**	**$420,390.6**	**$310,486.8**

Note: Data for funds that invest in other mutual funds were excluded from the series.

Redemptions Due to Exchanges by Investment Objective
(millions of dollars)

	1999	2000	2001
Total	$947,387.8	$1,145,418.6	$798,078.7
Aggressive Growth	$113,995.3	$166,005.9	$109,614.8
Growth	114,311.8	140,195.4	105,925.9
Sector	49,545.6	71,194.5	44,848.7
World Equity–Emerging Markets	2,855.9	5,404.3	2,181.2
World Equity–Global	39,378.7	50,108.0	25,665.2
World Equity–International	52,360.5	73,367.8	44,847.3
World Equity–Regional	16,054.5	18,470.2	12,794.8
Growth and Income	75,772.2	87,097.2	52,766.4
Income Equity	14,920.0	16,099.5	7,195.8
Total Equity Funds	$479,194.5	$627,942.8	$405,840.1
Asset Allocation	$4,617.0	$4,296.7	$4,868.3
Balanced	12,257.0	15,230.5	7,501.1
Flexible Portfolio	3,952.9	3,870.9	2,969.5
Income–Mixed	4,736.1	4,642.6	1,875.7
Total Hybrid Funds	$25,563.0	$28,040.7	$17,214.6
Corporate Bond–General	$2,731.9	$2,496.9	$2,447.2
Corporate Bond–Intermediate-Term	6,304.2	4,399.2	4,463.8
Corporate Bond–Short-Term	5,213.9	4,699.1	6,961.0
High-Yield Bond	15,780.5	14,939.5	10,845.6
World Bond–Global General	1,463.9	1,443.6	976.7
World Bond–Global Short-Term	193.8	113.4	119.8
World Bond–Other	416.4	358.5	453.8
Government Bond–General	7,160.0	4,791.9	7,934.1
Government Bond–Intermediate-Term	4,734.4	3,430.7	4,538.2
Government Bond–Short-Term	6,726.5	5,202.2	3,877.3
Government Bond–Mortgage-Backed	8,221.1	8,393.5	5,745.2
Strategic Income	8,103.7	10,180.6	12,047.6
State Municipal Bond–General	8,647.1	5,609.2	5,308.0
State Municipal Bond–Short-Term	675.3	287.4	208.5
National Municipal Bond–General	16,789.4	10,000.7	10,562.5
National Municipal Bond–Short-Term	3,071.7	2,127.5	2,001.7
Total Bond Funds	$96,233.8	$78,473.9	$78,491.0
Taxable Money Market–Government	$46,285.4	$45,995.7	$36,792.4
Taxable Money Market–Non-Government	281,290.9	347,708.5	242,099.9
National Tax-Exempt Money Market	13,640.3	11,682.5	10,453.9
State Tax-Exempt Money Market	5,179.9	5,574.5	7,186.8
Total Money Market Funds	$346,396.5	$410,961.2	$296,533.0

Note: Data for funds that invest in other mutual funds were excluded from the series.

Net Sales Due to Exchanges by Investment Objective
(millions of dollars)

	1999	2000	2001
Total	$2,552.6	$4,334.0	($739.2)
Aggressive Growth	$8,122.3	$27,315.3	($2,534.0)
Growth	14,650.3	22,122.6	(12,589.3)
Sector	4,181.3	13,289.2	(3,176.3)
World Equity–Emerging Markets	358.0	(149.7)	(322.0)
World Equity–Global	(649.6)	2,190.9	(4,280.4)
World Equity–International	782.6	2,475.8	(3,183.1)
World Equity–Regional	301.4	(2,790.0)	(1,996.0)
Growth and Income	(7,324.7)	(29,167.5)	(1,506.2)
Income Equity	(7,283.6)	(9,185.4)	1,235.7
Total Equity Funds	**$13,138.0**	**$26,101.2**	**($28,351.6)**
Asset Allocation	($2,149.8)	($1,361.7)	($256.8)
Balanced	(4,179.0)	(8,600.4)	1,313.0
Flexible Portfolio	(1,678.5)	(1,530.2)	(986.1)
Income–Mixed	(3,231.6)	(3,075.3)	194.9
Total Hybrid Funds	**($11,238.9)**	**($14,567.6)**	**$265.0**
Corporate Bond–General	($551.4)	($473.7)	$896.5
Corporate Bond–Intermediate-Term	(678.1)	(937.3)	2,376.2
Corporate Bond–Short-Term	484.4	(990.8)	540.9
High-Yield Bond	(2,780.3)	(4,671.2)	247.4
World Bond–Global General	(491.2)	(484.0)	(262.0)
World Bond–Global Short-Term	(89.2)	(20.2)	(12.1)
World Bond–Other	(127.0)	(78.5)	(113.9)
Government Bond–General	(1,374.4)	(1,176.7)	374.3
Government Bond–Intermediate-Term	(472.1)	(579.8)	1,139.5
Government Bond–Short-Term	(1,483.0)	(2,185.9)	471.8
Government Bond–Mortgage-Backed	(370.9)	(1,160.6)	2,614.1
Strategic Income	(1,502.1)	(2,019.6)	4,168.8
State Municipal Bond–General	(2,263.6)	(488.1)	(221.8)
State Municipal Bond–Short-Term	(74.3)	(99.7)	71.9
National Municipal Bond–General	(2,784.9)	(1,008.4)	675.6
National Municipal Bond–Short-Term	(20.6)	(254.5)	426.4
Total Bond Funds	**($14,578.7)**	**($16,629.0)**	**$13,393.6**
Taxable Money Market–Government	$3,742.1	($689.8)	$3,873.5
Taxable Money Market–Non-Government	8,222.5	8,769.2	10,540.0
National Tax-Exempt Money Market	2,610.2	721.2	576.3
State Tax-Exempt Money Market	657.4	628.8	(1,036.0)
Total Money Market Funds	**$15,232.2**	**$9,429.4**	**$13,953.8**

Note: Data for funds that invest in other mutual funds were excluded from the series.

Section Five: Institutional Investors in the U.S. Industry

Assets of Major Institutions and Financial Intermediaries

(millions of dollars)

	1995	1996	1997	1998	1999	2000	2001
Depository Institutions	$5,817,216.0	$6,072,189.0	$6,557,007.0	$7,122,098.0	$7,546,269.0	$8,121,935.0	$8,679,041.0
Commercial Banks[1]	4,493,798.0	4,710,397.0	5,174,550.0	5,642,181.0	5,980,330.0	6,462,246.0	6,875,570.0
Credit Unions[2]	310,661.0	330,114.0	353,831.0	391,483.0	414,527.0	441,066.0	505,501.0
Savings Institutions[3]	1,012,757.0	1,031,678.0	1,028,626.0	1,088,434.0	1,151,412.0	1,218,623.0	1,297,970.0
Life Insurance	2,063,613.0	2,246,289.0	2,514,802.0	2,769,522.0	3,067,922.0	3,135,664.0	3,305,830.0
Investment Institutions	5,391,783.8	6,352,553.8	7,982,754.7	9,677,672.8	11,391,977.8	11,540,293.7	7,105,140.8
Bank-Administered Trusts[4]	2,444,822.9	2,684,453.4	3,364,446.6	3,999,320.7	4,380,797.8	4,437,206.7[p]	N/A
Closed-End Investment Companies	135,668.7	142,299.6	150,107.5	153,142.8	164,840.8	138,420.0	130,164.9[p]
Mutual Funds[5]	2,811,292.2	3,525,800.8	4,468,200.6	5,525,209.3	6,846,339.2	6,964,667.0	6,974,975.9

[1]Includes U.S.-chartered commercial banks, foreign banking offices in the U.S., bank holding companies, and banks in affiliated areas.

[2]Includes only federal or federally insured state credit unions serving natural persons.

[3]Includes mutual savings banks, federal savings banks, and savings & loan associations.

[4]Reflects only discretionary trusts and agencies.

[5]Includes short-term funds; excludes funds of funds.

[p]Preliminary data

N/A=Not available

Sources: Federal Reserve Board, Federal Financial Institutions Examination Council, and Investment Company Institute

Assets of Fiduciary, Business, and Other Institutional Investors[1]

(millions of dollars)

Equity, Hybrid, and Bond Funds

	1999	2000	2001P
Fiduciaries (Banks and Individuals Serving as Trustees, Guardians, and Administrators)	$394,534.2	$396,800.1	$359,084.9
Business Organizations	1,866,085.7	1,791,300.9	1,575,337.9
Business Corporations	133,696.6	129,967.7	107,788.7
Retirement Plans	1,123,362.3	1,068,811.8	953,976.1
Insurance Companies and Other Financial Institutions	609,026.8	592,521.4	513,573.1
Nonprofit Organizations	54,007.8	61,101.8	69,884.3
Other Institutional Investors Not Classified[2]	28,538.4	29,272.5	23,225.9
Total	$2,343,166.0	$2,278,475.3	$2,027,533.0

Note: Reporters of institutional data represented 82.2% of total assets in 1999, 84.4% in 2000, and 76.4% in 2001.

Taxable Money Market Funds

	1999	2000	2001P
Fiduciaries (Banks and Individuals Serving as Trustees, Guardians, and Administrators)	$225,809.7	$265,422.6	$354,941.1
Business Organizations	423,889.5	477,209.5	662,510.3
Business Corporations	174,298.6	208,433.0	302,164.4
Retirement Plans	82,596.2	84,677.2	89,419.4
Insurance Companies and Other Financial Institutions	166,994.8	184,099.4	270,926.4
Nonprofit Organizations	19,546.7	23,293.9	48,226.5
Other Institutional Investors Not Classified[2]	31,347.6	37,608.2	24,513.4
Total	$700,593.5	$803,534.2	$1,090,191.3

Note: Reporters of institutional data represented 59.6% of total assets in 1999, 64.1% in 2000, and 65.4% in 2001.

Tax-Exempt Money Market Funds

	1999	2000	2001P
Fiduciaries (Banks and Individuals Serving as Trustees, Guardians, and Administrators)	$36,783.2	$46,234.2	$54,184.8
Business Organizations	20,130.8	21,465.8	23,690.7
Business Corporations	11,327.0	11,456.5	15,432.3
Retirement Plans	742.7	627.3	843.7
Insurance Companies and Other Financial Institutions	8,061.1	9,382.0	7,414.7
Nonprofit Organizations	1,009.4	1,454.6	9,801.3
Other Institutional Investors Not Classified[2]	1,214.0	2,524.5	2,663.9
Total	$59,137.3	$71,679.1	$90,340.6

Note: Reporters of institutional data represented 64.3% of total net assets in 1999, 66.2% in 2000, and 65.7% in 2001.

[1]*Data for funds that invest in other mutual funds were excluded from the series.*
[2]*Includes institutional assets for which no determination of classification can be made.*
P*Preliminary data*
Note: Components may not sum to the total due to rounding.

Assets of Fiduciary, Business, and Other Institutional Investors in Taxable Money Market Funds by Type of Fund
(millions of dollars)

	Retail			Institutional		
	1999	2000	2001P	1999	2000	2001P
Fiduciaries (Banks and Individuals Serving as Trustees, Guardians, and Administrators)	$82,006.0	$100,416.6	$111,584.8	$143,803.7	$165,006.0	$243,356.3
Business Organizations	145,046.4	138,726.1	155,848.8	278,843.1	338,483.4	506,661.5
Business Corporations	55,962.3	55,346.6	59,260.9	118,336.3	153,086.4	242,903.5
Retirement Plans	49,556.6	47,936.1	51,258.2	33,039.6	36,741.1	38,161.2
Insurance Companies and Other Financial Institutions	39,527.5	35,443.5	45,329.6	127,467.3	148,655.8	225,596.8
Nonprofit Organizations	6,173.6	6,589.9	8,653.2	13,373.1	16,704.1	39,573.3
Other Institutional Investors Not Classified*	9,609.8	11,358.7	9,284.7	21,737.8	26,249.5	15,228.7
Total	$242,835.9	$257,091.3	$285,371.5	$457,757.7	$546,443.0	$804,819.8

*Includes institutional assets for which no determination of classification can be made.

PPreliminary data

Note: Data for funds that invest in other mutual funds were excluded from the series. Components may not sum to the total due to rounding.

Worldwide Assets of Open-End Funds

(millions of U.S. dollars)

NON-USA COUNTRIES	1996	1997	1998	1999	2000	2001[a]
Argentina	$1,869	$5,247	$6,930	$6,990	$7,425	$7,357
Australia	47,761	42,909	44,124[b]	N/A	341,955	304,145
Austria[c]	39,543	44,930	63,772	75,730	78,429	53,927
Belgium	29,247	33,658	56,339	65,461	70,313	64,449
Brazil	103,786	108,606	118,687	117,758	148,538	126,833
Canada[c]	154,529	197,985	213,451	269,825	279,511	244,025
Chile	2,934	4,549	2,910	4,091	4,431[d]	4,743
Costa Rica	N/A	N/A	N/A	N/A	919	1,428
Czech Republic	N/A	361	556	1,473	1,990	1,644
Denmark	9,338	13,037	19,450	27,545	32,457	30,462
Finland	2,510	3,534	5,695	10,318	12,698	12,131
France	534,145	495,774	626,154	656,132	721,973	700,944
Germany	137,860	146,888	195,701	237,312	238,029	192,617
Greece	15,788	25,759	32,194	36,397	29,154	21,885
Hong Kong	41,017	58,456	98,767	182,265	195,924	183,030
Hungary	N/A	713	1,476	1,725	1,953	2,202
India	9,717[e]	9,353	8,685	13,065	13,831	13,490
Ireland[f]	7,735	22,729	22,520[g]	95,135	136,940	166,979[h]
Italy	129,992	209,410	439,701	478,530	424,014	352,415
Japan	420,103	311,335	376,533	502,752	431,996	465,962
Korea	N/A	N/A	N/A	167,177	110,613	137,056
Luxembourg	338,236	390,623	N/A	659,284	747,117	694,183
Mexico	N/A	N/A	N/A	19,468	18,488	27,608
Netherlands[c]	67,147	70,373	87,996	102,492	94,106	N/A
New Zealand[c]	7,686	7,519	7,250	8,502	7,802	6,796
Norway	9,930	13,058	11,148	15,107	16,228	13,861
Philippines	N/A	N/A	N/A	117	108	170
Poland	475	541	517	762	1,546	1,317
Portugal	17,079	15,472	23,299	20,574	16,588	15,840
Romania	N/A	N/A	N/A	N/A	8	11
Russia	6	41	29	177	177	249
South Africa	9,354	12,688	12,160	18,235	16,921	15,557
Spain	144,134	177,192	238,917	207,603	172,438	154,670
Sweden	34,981	45,452	54,923	83,250	78,074	56,157
Switzerland	48,166	53,444	69,151	82,512	83,063	72,556
Taiwan	8,351[e]	12,365	20,310	31,153	32,074	43,641
United Kingdom[i]	201,304	235,683	283,711	370,962	387,149	333,887
TOTAL NON-USA	$2,574,723	$2,769,684	$3,143,056	$4,569,879	$4,954,980	$4,524,227
USA[i] (long-term)	2,623,994	3,409,315	4,173,531	5,233,194	5,119,386	4,252,647
(short-term)	901,807	1,058,886	1,351,678	1,613,146	1,845,281	2,161,639
TOTAL USA	$3,525,801	$4,468,201	$5,525,209	$6,846,340	$6,964,667	$6,414,286
TOTAL WORLD	$6,100,524	$7,237,885	$8,668,265	$11,416,219	$11,919,647	$10,938,513

[a]As of September 30, 2001, unless otherwise noted.
[b]As of September 30, 1998.
[c]Includes real estate funds.
[d]As of June 30, 2000.
[e]As of June 30, 1996.
[f]Approximately 95 percent relates to life assurance-linked funds; the other 5 percent are unit investment trusts. International Financial Service Center funds are not included.
[g]As of March 31, 1998.
[h]As of August 31, 2001.
[i]Funds of funds not included.
N/A=Not available
Note: Comparison of annual total assets across countries is not recommended because reporting coverage, dates, and definitions are not consistent.
Sources: European Federation of Investment Funds and Companies, Investment Company Institute

Worldwide Number of Open-End Funds

	1996	1997	1998	1999	2000	2001[a]
NON-USA COUNTRIES						
Argentina	149	195	229	224	226	231
Australia	1,047	488	569[b]	N/A	N/A	N/A
Austria[c]	517	625	821	1,316	1,733	752
Belgium	330	458	631	784	918	1,008
Brazil	1,143	1,502	1,601	1,760	2,097	2,342
Canada[c]	954	1,023	1,130	1,328	1,627	1,813
Chile	77	92	102	116	126[d]	167
Costa Rica	N/A	N/A	N/A	N/A	122	136
Czech Republic	N/A	47	56	62	70	57
Denmark	189	222	240	304	394	438
Finland	62	81	114	176	241	263
France	5,379	5,797	6,274	6,511	7,144	7,473
Germany	641	717	848	895	987	1,061
Greece	148	162	179	208	265	270
Hong Kong	708	772	712	832	976	963
Hungary	N/A	37	66	87	86	89
India	42[e]	64	97	155	243	292
Ireland[f]	260	260	260[g]	N/A	1,344	1,592
Italy	531	626	703	823	967	1,038
Japan	5,879	5,203	4,534	3,444	2,793	2,744
Korea[h]	N/A	N/A	N/A	13,606	8,242	7,497
Luxembourg	3,234	4,064	N/A	5,023	6,084	6,508
Mexico	N/A	N/A	N/A	280	305	326
Netherlands[c]	179	289	334	348	494	N/A
New Zealand[c]	551	629	633	622	607	606
Norway	188	233	264	309	380	397
Philippines	N/A	N/A	N/A	15	18	20
Poland	5	20	38	62	77	92
Portugal	151	163	197	226	195	203
Romania	N/A	N/A	N/A	N/A	16	20
Russia	4	18	28	27	37	52
South Africa	107	149	191	260	334	395
Spain	958	1,456	1,866	2,150	2,422	2,501
Sweden	316	344	366	412	509	502
Switzerland	251	296	325	348	323	311
Taiwan	82[e]	127	174	318	288	315
United Kingdom[i]	1,452	1,455	1,541	1,594	1,937	1,961
TOTAL NON-USA	**25,534**	**27,614**	**25,123**	**44,625**	**44,627**	**44,435**
USA[i] (long-term)	5,260	5,671	6,288	6,746	7,116	7,285
(short-term)	988	1,013	1,026	1,045	1,039	1,015
TOTAL USA	**6,248**	**6,684**	**7,314**	**7,791**	**8,155**	**8,300**
TOTAL WORLD	**31,782**	**34,298**	**32,437**	**52,416**	**52,782**	**52,735**

[a]*As of September 30, 2001.*
[b]*As of September 30, 1998.*
[c]*Includes real estate funds.*
[d]*As of June 30, 2000.*
[e]*As of June 30,1996.*
[f]*Approximately 95 percent relates to life assurance-linked funds; the other 5 percent are unit investment trusts. International Financial Service Center funds are not included.*
[g]*As of March 31, 1998.*
[h]*Number of funds does not include bank trust funds.*
[i]*Funds of funds not included.*
N/A = Not available
Note: Comparison of annual total assets across countries is not recommended because reporting coverage, dates, and definitions are not consistent.
Sources: European Federation of Investment Funds and Companies, Investment Company Institute

Section Seven: Other U.S. Investment Companies

Outstanding Assets and Number of Closed-End Funds by Type of Fund

(millions of dollars)

	1997 Assets Outstanding	1997 Number of Funds	1998 Assets Outstanding	1998 Number of Funds	1999 Assets Outstanding	1999 Number of Funds	2000 Assets Outstanding	2000 Number of Funds	2001p Assets Outstanding	2001p Number of Funds
Convertible	$1,151.3	10	$1,156.1	10	$1,319.5	9	$1,005.1	8	$986.9	8
Taxable Bond	26,152.1	101	32,546.9	108	27,516.9	99	26,142.9	96	21,726.4	89
Municipal Bond – National	41,944.6	99	43,032.1	103	41,926.4	106	45,481.1	107	44,299.0	96
Municipal Bond – Single State	17,802.0	101	18,851.9	108	20,641.7	132	20,609.1	117	25,335.1	131
Equity	22,303.6	48	23,455.0	48	25,254.1	50	24,340.2	55	21,839.7	51
TOTAL DOMESTIC	$109,353.6	359	$119,042.0	377	$116,658.6	396	$117,578.4	383	$114,187.1	375
Multi Country Debt	$2,095.7	9	$1,493.7	8	$1,715.7	9	$1,671.9	9	1,510.8	7
Single Country Debt	2,407.5	3	1,898.1	3	1,675.5	1	1,481.6	2	1,296.6	2
Multi Country Equity	18,864.5	29	16,792.9	27	27,735.3	22	3,639.9	21	2,479.4	18
Single Country Equity	8,961.3	52	6,730.3	47	9,960.4	44	7,134.6	44	5,095.7	36
TOTAL FOREIGN	$32,329.0	93	$26,915.0	85	$41,086.9	76	$13,928.0	76	$10,382.5	63
Global Debt	$6,977.0	18	$5,945.7	17	$5,768.7	17	$5,562.0	18	5,130.1	15
Global Equity	1,447.9	10	1,240.1	7	1,326.6	6	1,351.6	6	465.2	5
TOTAL GLOBAL	$8,424.9	28	$7,185.8	24	$7,095.3	23	$6,913.6	24	$5,595.3	20
TOTAL	$150,107.5	480	$153,142.8	486	$164,840.8	495	$138,420.0	483	$130,164.9	458

pPreliminary data

New Deposits of Unit Investment Trusts by Type of Trust
(thousands of dollars)

	Total Trusts	Equity Trusts	Tax-Free Debt Trusts	Taxable Debt Trusts
2000				
January	$6,291,814	$6,157,018	$116,732	$18,064
February	6,301,246	6,202,928	82,882	15,436
March	5,692,058	5,595,817	83,217	13,024
April	2,856,170	2,800,958	46,150	9,062
May	2,983,278	2,908,751	60,467	14,060
June	3,217,314	3,096,056	106,565	14,693
July	3,998,418	3,801,850	70,421	126,147
August	2,995,024	2,662,262	100,308	232,454
September	3,372,246	3,059,590	56,801	255,855
October	2,810,277	2,479,739	66,392	264,146
November	1,817,454	1,742,841	56,461	18,152
December	2,164,930	2,111,854	36,313	16,763
Total	**$44,500,229**	**$42,619,664**	**$882,709**	**$997,856**
2001				
January	$3,541,406	$3,369,012	$126,342	$46,052
February	2,772,263	2,615,131	116,193	40,939
March	1,727,175	1,515,251	131,550	80,374
April	1,194,417	1,053,969	112,524	27,924
May	1,515,211	1,327,890	160,109	27,212
June	1,294,269	1,131,442	125,894	36,933
July	2,382,014	2,206,361	145,041	30,612
August	998,582	787,601	161,484	49,497
September	741,680	579,952	112,244	49,484
October	1,004,705	817,882	113,679	73,144
November	965,114	764,169	141,487	59,458
December	912,410	758,085	103,794	50,531
Total	**$19,049,246**	**$16,926,745**	**$1,550,341**	**$572,160**

Section Seven: Other U.S. Investment Companies

Annual Assets, Net Issuance, and Number of Exchange-Traded Equity Index Funds by Type of Fund
(millions of dollars)

	Domestic			Global/International			Total		
	Assets (End of Period)	Net Issuance	Number of Funds (End of Period)	Assets (End of Period)	Net Issuance	Number of Funds (End of Period)	Assets (End of Period)	Net Issuance	Number of Funds (End of Period)
1993	$464	$450	1	–	–	–	$464	$450	1
1994	424	(28)	1	–	–	–	424	(28)	1
1995	1,052	441	2	–	–	–	1,052	441	2
1996	2,158	844	2	$243	$246	17	2,401	1,088	19
1997	6,203	3,142	2	499	298	17	6,702	3,439	19
1998	14,546	5,599	12	1,018	425	17	15,564	6,025	29
1999	31,876	11,763	13	1,986	399	17	33,862	12,164	30
2000	63,544	41,831	55	2,041	545	25	65,585	42,378	80
2001	79,977	29,646	68	3,016	1,367	34	82,993	31,012	102

Note: Components may not sum to total because of rounding.

Sources: Strategic Insight and Investment Company Institute

Section Seven: Other U.S. Investment Companies

Monthly Assets, Net Issuance, and Number of Exchange-Traded Equity Index Funds by Type of Fund

(millions of dollars)

	Domestic			Global/International			Total		
	Assets (End of Period)	Net Issuance	Number of Funds (End of Period)	Assets (End of Period)	Net Issuance	Number of Funds (End of Period)	Assets (End of Period)	Net Issuance	Number of Funds (End of Period)
2000									
January	$30,824	$223	13	$1,902	$42	17	$32,726	$265	30
February	31,907	399	13	1,897	(21)	17	33,804	379	30
March	34,748	(174)	13	2,045	53	17	36,793	(120)	30
April	36,268	3,849	13	1,964	47	17	38,232	3,896	30
May	39,468	5,068	27	1,860	(49)	17	41,328	5,019	44
June	44,102	2,564	36	1,988	99	20	46,091	2,663	56
July	43,085	(21)	46	1,955	70	23	45,041	49	69
August	46,683	(847)	46	1,932	(73)	23	48,615	(920)	69
September	47,792	4,304	52	1,909	86	24	49,701	4,390	76
October	54,646	7,959	55	1,900	63	24	56,546	8,022	79
November	54,479	7,922	55	1,869	46	24	56,348	7,968	79
December	63,544	10,585	55	2,041	182	25	65,585	10,767	80
2001									
January	$70,100	$2,395	56	$2,034	($53)	25	$72,134	$2,342	81
February	62,428	3,204	57	1,915	10	25	64,343	3,214	82
March	64,205	8,898	58	1,800	16	25	66,006	8,914	83
April	71,413	(365)	59	1,917	11	25	73,330	(353)	84
May	70,854	(289)	60	1,919	42	25	72,773	(248)	85
June	73,643	3,350	60	1,917	78	25	75,560	3,428	85
July	73,678	2,593	66	1,842	(14)	25	75,520	2,578	85
August	69,995	2,375	66	2,090	305	26	72,085	2,680	91
September	62,401	1,628	66	1,944	98	26	64,345	1,726	92
October	67,173	615	67	2,248	246	29	69,421	861	92
November	76,265	2,031	67	2,581	231	34	78,846	2,262	96
December	79,977	3,211	68	3,016	397	34	82,993	3,608	101

Note: Components may not sum to total because of rounding.

Data Points

(trillions of dollars)

	Equity Funds	Hybrid Funds	Bond Funds	Money Market Funds	Total
1990	$0.239	$0.036	$0.291	$0.498	$1.065
1991	$0.405	$0.052	$0.394	$0.542	$1.393
1992	$0.514	$0.078	$0.504	$0.546	$1.643
1993	$0.741	$0.145	$0.619	$0.565	$2.070
1994	$0.853	$0.164	$0.527	$0.611	$2.155
1995	$1.249	$0.210	$0.599	$0.753	$2.811
1996	$1.726	$0.253	$0.645	$0.902	$3.526
1997	$2.368	$0.317	$0.724	$1.059	$4.468
1998	$2.978	$0.365	$0.831	$1.352	$5.525
1999	$4.042	$0.379	$0.812	$1.613	$6.846
2000	$3.962	$0.346	$0.811	$1.845	$6.965
2001	$3.418	$0.346	$0.925	$2.285	$6.975

(trillions of dollars)

	Year-End 1989 Mutual Fund Assets	Cumulative Net New Cash Flow	Cumulative Performance	Cumulative Newly Reporting Funds	Total Mutual Fund Assets
1990	$0.981	$0.044	$0.012	$0.028	$1.065
1991	0.981	0.156	0.159	0.098	1.393
1992	0.981	0.312	0.222	0.129	1.643
1993	0.981	0.539	0.372	0.178	2.070
1994	0.981	0.623	0.316	0.236	2.155
1995	0.981	0.835	0.692	0.303	2.811
1996	0.981	1.156	0.985	0.403	3.526
1997	0.981	1.530	1.466	0.491	4.468
1998	0.981	2.008	1.985	0.552	5.525
1999	0.981	2.371	2.858	0.637	6.846
2000	0.981	2.759	2.502	0.723	6.965
2001	0.981	3.264	1.952	0.778	6.975

*All total asset figures plotted in this chart represent the cumulative contribution of newly reporting funds, net new cash flow, and fund investment performance from year-end 1989 through the end of each year plotted. Asset levels plotted also include year-end 1989 assets of $981 billion.

Note: Components may not sum to total mutual fund assets due to rounding.

Page 25—Net Purchases of Stocks and Bonds by Households, 1990–2001

(billions of dollars)

	Net Purchases Made Through Mutual Funds	Net Purchases Made Outside Mutual Funds
1990	$36.5	$191.5
1991	140.6	90.5
1992	169.6	90.5
1993	266.3	(86.9)
1994	117.5	101.7
1995	133.6	(104.3)
1996	277.9	(123.1)
1997	299.9	(366.5)
1998	325.9	(361.9)
1999	192.6	(136.9)
2000	234.0	(662.2)
2001	250.0	(426.6)

Sources: Federal Reserve Board and Investment Company Institute

Page 30—Share of U.S. Nonfinancial Business Short-Term Assets* Held Through Money Market Funds, 1990–2001

(percent of total)

1990	6.3
1991	7.2
1992	10.2
1993	8.8
1994	9.6
1995	12.9
1996	12.7
1997	14.4
1998	16.7
1999	17.9
2000	20.6
2001	28.4

*Business short-term assets consist of foreign deposits, checkable deposits, time and savings deposits, money market funds, repurchase agreements, and commercial paper.

Sources: Federal Reserve Board and Investment Company Institute

Page 53 — Average 401(k) Account Balance by Age and Tenure, 2000

(dollars)

Age Cohort	Participant Job Tenure (years)					
	0 to 2	>2 to 5	>5 to 10	>10 to 20	>20 to 30	> 30
20s	$3,778	$7,952	$12,969			
30s	8,454	16,159	30,253	$49,321		
40s	12,145	20,685	39,604	78,276	$89,874	
50s	14,474	22,790	44,832	91,096	134,645	$138,627
60s	16,132	22,699	43,450	87,050	126,466	177,289

Source: Tabulations from EBRI/ICI Participant-Directed Retirement Plan Data Collection Project

Glossary of Mutual Fund Terms

For an explanation of fund types, see pages 8–11.

Adviser–An organization employed by a mutual fund to give professional advice on the fund's investments and asset management practices (also called the investment adviser).

After-Tax Return–The total return of a fund after the effects of taxes on distributions and/or redemptions have been assessed. Funds are required by federal securities law to calculate after-tax returns using standardized formulas based upon the highest tax rates. (Consequently, they are not representative of the after-tax returns of most mutual fund shareholders.) These standardized after-tax returns are irrelevant for shareholders in tax-deferred retirement accounts.

Annual and Semiannual Reports–Summaries that a mutual fund sends to its shareholders that discuss the fund's performance over a certain period and identify the securities in the fund's portfolio on a specific date.

Appreciation–An increase in an investment's value.

Asked or Offering Price–(As seen in some mutual fund newspaper listings.) The price at which a mutual fund's shares can be purchased. The asked or offering price includes the current net asset value per share plus any sales charge.

Assets–The current dollar value of the pool of money shareholders have invested in a fund.

Automatic Reinvestment–A fund service giving shareholders the option to purchase additional shares using dividend and capital gain distributions.

Average Portfolio Maturity–The average maturity of all the bonds in a bond fund's portfolio.

Bear Market–A period during which securities prices in a particular market (such as the stock market) are generally falling.

Bid or Sell Price—The price at which a mutual fund's shares are redeemed, or bought back, by the fund. The price is usually the current net asset value per share. See Net Asset Value (NAV).

Bond—A debt security, or IOU, issued by a company, municipality, or government agency. A bond investor lends money to the issuer and, in exchange, the issuer promises to repay the loan amount on a specified maturity date; the issuer usually pays the bondholder periodic interest payments over the life of the loan.

Broker-Dealer—A firm that buys and sells mutual fund shares and other securities from and to investors.

Bull Market—A period during which securities prices in a particular market (such as the stock market) are generally rising.

Capital Gain Distribution—Profits distributed to shareholders resulting from the sale of securities held in the fund's portfolio for more than one year.

Closed-End Fund—A type of investment company that has a fixed number of shares which are publicly traded. The price of a closed-end fund's shares fluctuates based on investor supply and demand. Closed-end funds are not required to redeem shares and have managed portfolios.

Commission—A fee paid by an investor to a broker or other sales agent for investment advice and assistance.

Compounding—Earnings on an investment's earnings. Over time, compounding can produce significant growth in the value of an investment.

Contingent Deferred Sales Charge (CDSC)—A fee imposed when shares are redeemed (sold back to the fund) during the first few years of ownership.

Credit Risk—The possibility that a bond issuer may not be able to pay interest and repay its debt.

Custodian—An organization, usually a bank, that holds the securities and other assets of a mutual fund.

Depreciation—A decline in an investment's value.

Distribution—1) The payment of dividends and capital gains, or 2) a term used to describe a method of selling to the public.

Diversification – The practice of investing broadly across a number of securities to reduce risk.

Dollar-Cost Averaging – The practice of investing a fixed amount of money at regular intervals, regardless of whether the securities markets are declining or rising.

Exchange Privilege – A fund option enabling shareholders to transfer their investments from one fund to another within the same fund family as their needs or objectives change. Typically, fund companies allow exchanges several times a year for a low or no fee.

Exchange-Traded Fund (ETF) – An investment company with shares that trade intraday on stock exchanges at market-determined prices. Investors may buy or sell ETF shares through a broker just as they would the shares of any publicly traded company.

Ex-Dividend Date – With regard to mutual funds, this is the day on which declared distributions (dividends or capital gains) are deducted from the fund's assets before it calculates its net asset value (NAV). The NAV per share will drop by the amount of the distribution per share.

Expense Ratio – A fund's cost of doing business — disclosed in the prospectus — expressed as a percentage of its assets.

Face Value – The amount that a bond's issuer must repay at the maturity date.

Family of Funds – A group of mutual funds, each typically with its own investment objective, managed and distributed by the same company.

401(k) Plan – An employer-sponsored retirement plan that enables employees to make tax-deferred contributions from their salaries to the plan.

403(b) Plan – An employer-sponsored retirement plan that enables employees of universities, public schools, and nonprofit organizations to make tax-deferred contributions from their salaries to the plan.

457 Plan – An employer-sponsored retirement plan that enables employees of state and local governments and other tax-exempt employers to make tax-deferred contributions from their salaries to the plan.

Hedge Fund – A private investment pool for wealthy investors that, unlike a mutual fund, is exempt from SEC regulation.

Hybrid Fund–A mutual fund that invests in a combination of stocks, bonds, and other securities.

Income–Dividends, interest, and/or short-term capital gains paid to a mutual fund's shareholders. Income is earned on a fund's investment portfolio after deducting operating expenses.

Individual Retirement Account (IRA)–An investor-established, tax-deferred account set up to hold and invest funds until retirement.

Inflation Risk–The risk that a portion of an investment's return may be eliminated by inflation.

Interest Rate Risk–The possibility that a bond's or bond mutual fund's value will decrease due to rising interest rates.

Investment Adviser–An organization employed by a mutual fund to give professional advice on the fund's investments and asset management practices.

Investment Company–A corporation, trust, or partnership that invests pooled shareholder dollars in securities appropriate to the organization's objective. Mutual funds, closed-end funds, unit investment trusts, and exchange-traded funds are the four main types of investment companies.

Investment Objective–The goal that an investor and mutual fund pursue together (e.g., current income, long-term capital growth, etc.).

Issuer–The company, municipality, or government agency that issues a security, such as stocks, bonds, or money market instruments.

Large-Cap Stocks–Stocks of large-capitalization companies, which are generally considered to be companies whose total outstanding shares are valued at $10 billion or more.

Liquidity–The ability to gain ready access to invested money. Mutual funds are liquid because their shares can be redeemed for current value (which may be more or less than the original cost) on any business day.

Long-Term Funds–A mutual fund industry designation for all funds other than money market funds. Long-term funds are broadly divided into equity (stock), bond, and hybrid funds.

Management Fee–The amount paid by a mutual fund to the investment adviser for its services.

Maturity–The date by which an issuer promises to repay a bond's face value.

Mutual Fund–An investment company that buys a portfolio of securities selected by a professional investment adviser to meet a specified financial goal. Investors buy shares in a fund, which represent ownership in all the fund's securities. A mutual fund stands ready to buy back its shares at their current net asset value, which is the total market value of the fund's investment portfolio, minus its liabilities, divided by the number of shares outstanding. Most mutual funds continuously offer new shares to investors.

National Association of Securities Dealers, Inc. (NASD)–A self-regulatory organization with authority over firms that distribute mutual fund shares as well as other securities.

Net Asset Value (NAV)–The per-share value of a mutual fund, found by subtracting the fund's liabilities from its assets and dividing by the number of shares outstanding. Mutual funds calculate their NAVs at least once daily.

No-Load Fund–A mutual fund whose shares are sold without a sales commission and without a 12b-1 fee of more than .25 percent per year.

Open-End Investment Company–The legal name for a mutual fund, indicating that it stands ready to redeem (buy back) its shares from investors.

Operating Expenses–Business costs paid from a fund's assets before earnings are distributed to shareholders. These include management fees, 12b-1 fees, and other expenses.

Payroll Deduction Plan–An arrangement that some employers offer employees to accumulate mutual fund shares. Employees authorize their employer to deduct a specified amount from their salaries at stated times and transfer the proceeds to the fund.

Pooling–The basic concept behind mutual funds in which a fund aggregates the assets of investors who share common financial goals. A fund uses the investment pool to buy a diversified portfolio of investments, and each mutual fund share purchased represents ownership in all the fund's underlying securities.

Portfolio—A collection of securities owned by an individual or an institution (such as a mutual fund) that may include stocks, bonds, and money market securities.

Portfolio Manager—A specialist employed by a mutual fund's adviser to invest the fund's assets in accordance with predetermined investment objectives.

Portfolio Turnover—A measure of the trading activity in a fund's investment portfolio—how often securities are bought and sold by a fund.

Prepayment Risk—The possibility that a bond owner will receive his or her principal investment back from the issuer prior to the bond's maturity date.

Principal—See Face Value.

Professional Management—The full-time, experienced team of professionals that decides what securities to buy, hold, and sell for a mutual fund portfolio.

Prospectus—The official document that describes a mutual fund to prospective investors. The prospectus contains information required by the SEC, such as investment objectives and policies, risks, services, and fees.

Quality—The creditworthiness of a bond issuer, which indicates the likelihood that it will be able to repay its debt.

Redeem—To cash in mutual fund shares by selling them back to the fund. Mutual fund shares may be redeemed on any business day. An investor receives the current share price, called net asset value, minus any deferred sales charge or redemption fee.

Redemption Price—The amount per share (shown as the "bid" in newspaper tables) that mutual fund shareholders receive when they cash in shares. The value of a fund's shares on any given day depends on the current market value of its underlying investment portfolio at that time.

Reinvestment Privilege—An option whereby mutual fund dividend and capital gain distributions automatically buy new fund shares.

Risk/Reward Tradeoff—The principle that an investment must offer higher potential returns as compensation for the likelihood of increased volatility.

Rollover—The shifting of an investor's assets from one qualified retirement plan to another—due to changing jobs, for instance—without a tax penalty.

Sales Charge or Load–An amount charged for the sale of some fund shares, usually those sold by brokers or other sales professionals. By regulation, a mutual fund sales charge may not exceed 8.5 percent of an investment purchase. The charge may vary depending on the amount invested and the fund chosen. A sales charge or load is reflected in the asked or offering price. See Asked or Offering Price.

Series Fund–A group of different mutual funds, each with its own investment objective and policies, that is structured as a single corporation or business trust.

Share Classes (e.g., Class A, Class B, etc.)–Represent ownership in the same fund, but with different fee charges. This enables shareholders to choose the type of fee structure that best suits their particular needs.

Shareholder–An investor who owns shares of a mutual fund or other company.

Short-Term Funds–Another term for money market funds.

Small-Cap Stocks–Stock of small-capitalization companies, which are generally considered to be companies whose total outstanding shares are valued at less than $1.6 billion.

Statement of Additional Information (SAI)–The supplementary document to a prospectus that contains more detailed information about a mutual fund; also known as "Part B" of the prospectus.

Stock–A share of ownership or equity in a corporation.

Total Return–A measure of a fund's performance that encompasses all elements of return: dividends, capital gain distributions, and changes in net asset value. Total return is the change in value of an investment over a given period, assuming reinvestment of any dividends and capital gain distributions, expressed as a percentage of the initial investment.

Transfer Agent–The organization employed by a mutual fund to prepare and maintain records relating to shareholder accounts.

12b-1 Fee–A mutual fund fee, named for the SEC rule that permits it, used to pay distribution costs, such as advertising and commissions paid to dealers. If a fund has a 12b-1 fee, it will be disclosed in the fee table of a fund's prospectus.

Underwriter–The organization that sells a mutual fund's shares to broker-dealers and investors.

Unit Investment Trust (UIT)–An investment company that buys and holds a fixed number of shares until the trust's termination date. When the trust is dissolved, proceeds are paid to shareholders. A UIT has an unmanaged portfolio. Like a mutual fund, shares of a UIT can be redeemed on any business day.

U.S. Securities and Exchange Commission (SEC)–The primary U.S. government agency responsible for the regulation of the day-to-day operations and disclosure obligations of mutual funds.

Variable Annuity–An investment contract sold by an insurance company; capital is accumulated, often through mutual fund investments, and converted to an income stream later, often at an investor's retirement.

Withdrawal Plan–A fund service allowing shareholders to receive income or principal payments from their fund account at regular intervals.

Yield–A measure of net income (dividends and interest) earned by the securities in a fund's portfolio less the fund's expenses during a specified period. A fund's yield is expressed as a percentage of the maximum offering price per share on a specified date.

Index

A

B

C

D

E